Out of the Box Golf

Exploring the Innovative and Unconventional

Steve Bullock

A sincere thank you to my family and friends for the encouragement, support, and feedback.

CONTENTS

INTRODUCTION

Humans tend toward conformity. The social pressure to approach tasks in the same way as they've always been done is strong and individuals that diverge from the masses are often exposed to a disproportionate level of mockery and shame in cases of failure. This paradox of innovation slows progress in all types of groups, sports teams, and among individual athletes. It's precisely for this reason certain methods and philosophies have been perpetuated through generations of golfers even if those approaches aren't the best or optimal. It creates a general reluctance to experiment, try new things, and test different ideas.

Swimming against the currents of conformity were the mavericks and innovators of golf history. A defining personality trait of these pioneers was a disregard for the perceptions and often persistent ridicule of other people. It's not that trailblazing golfers didn't respect and learn from others or golf history; to the contrary, many talked about in these pages are among the greatest students and scholars of the game. It's also not that these pioneers believed they were inherently smarter than anyone else, but they had experienced the epiphany that just because people have done something a certain way for a very long time doesn't mean it's the best way. To not care what other people think in this context means an athlete has broken, at least to some degree, the human tendency toward conformity, the fear of being different. These golfers were willing to challenge the conventional, venture into the unproven, open their minds to greater possibilities and, in the process, change the game forever.

What is generally considered unconventional in golf today is, in reality, more common than most are aware and, in many cases, is increasing in popularity among the game's greatest golfers. For example, 30 years ago innovations such as cross-handed putting, the claw grip, and long-shafted putting styles were nearly non-existent, but today those unconventional grips are used by over 40% of the top 50 players in the world, a number that is rising almost every year. Likewise, in the 1960s chipping was generally a low-trajectory, bump-and-run style of play, but today we often witness the open-faced, outside-in flop shot magic of Phil Mickelson and others around the green.

It might at first appear that most top players have textbook full swings, but a case-by-case analysis shows a majority of top players have a distinctive quirk, significant enough to be commonly called out by golf analysts as unique. These quirks are often erroneously viewed and belittled as flaws but should be considered essential elements to the success of the individual's personal swing.

They range from obvious examples like Jim Furyk's looping swing path and Nancy Lopez's unique takeaway to more subtle ones like Jordan Spieth's chicken elbow and Judy Rankin's strong grip. Examples reach back in history to Lee Trevino's scrappy fade, Arnold Palmer's lunging attack, and Moe Norman's sawed-off follow through. Bryson DeChambeau's single plane, machine-like swing and Brooke Henderson's choked down grip with feet-off-the-ground impact position are modern-day unconventional methods.

Of the top 20 players in the world, it could be argued a majority significantly deviates from the ideal swing in some way or another. Speaking of Bryson DeChambeau, Tiger Woods once said, "He has figured out a way to play this game his own way and he's very efficient at what he does and he's not afraid to think outside the box on how he can become better. If you look at all the great players of all-time, they figure out their own way."[1] That last part is worth repeating – the great players of all time figure out their own way. Along the same lines, Arnold Palmer famously said, "Swing your swing. Not some idea of a swing. Not a swing you saw on TV. Not that swing you wish you had. No, swing your swing. Capable of greatness. Prized only by you. Perfect in its imperfection. Swing your swing. I know I did."

The young Phil Mickelson unknowingly followed Arnold Palmer's advice when he picked up a plastic club and started swinging it lefty even though that was opposite his natural handedness. In what may be a surprise to many, the man the golf world endearingly knows as "lefty" is actually right-handed in every other life task – writing, throwing, and eating. Before Phil, however, there was Hall of Fame golfer and New Zealand native Bob Charles, likewise a natural righty who golfed left-handed. He amassed more than 70 wins worldwide during his career including the 1963 Open Championship. Charles once explained, "I don't consider myself left-handed at all, my left side is totally useless. I wear a right-handed glove, I stand on the right side of the ball, I hit the ball on the right side of the clubface and I hit the ball to my right, whereas all you other people have a left-handed glove and you hit it to your left. So why I'm called left-handed, I don't know."[2] Stated in such stunning simplicity, one can't help but sit in contemplative silence as a life-long paradigm and fundamental view of the world flips completely upside down. What if the conventional notion of how a right-handed person should hit a golf ball is completely wrong? Digging deeper into the subject reveals a shocking number of the greatest players in history golfed opposite of conventional handedness. In this regard, golf might be lagging behind other sports such as hockey, cricket, and baseball.

Pondering future possibilities, one might consider a world in which professionals become switch hitters, golfing both right-handed and left-handed in the same round, carrying in their bags an equal allotment of righty and lefty clubs. The justification for such an approach is based on the angled shot distribution of each method. Backed by data analysis of rounds played at Augusta National, the theoretical stroke advantage of a switch-hitting golfer could be as large as six strokes per tournament; possibly the largest, most durable competitive edge opportunity in golf today.

Unconventional and innovative methods are not limited to swings, but can be seen in training techniques, physical fitness, and equipment. Gary Player was decades ahead of his time by adhering to a strict physical fitness and nutrition regimen. Bernhard Langer, Greg Norman, Annika Sorenstam, Tiger Woods, and Dustin Johnson all pushed the bounds of physical fitness in their respective eras. Today it appears that the golf world is in for another step change of swing speed and strength led by Bryson DeChambeau.

In the realm of mental game tactics, Tiger's traditional Sunday red shirt may have amplified what was already an intimidating final day environment for other players. Studies have since demonstrated across many sports that teams wearing red uniforms have a higher winning percentage than any other color of jersey. It held true even when uniforms were randomly assigned in the 2004 Olympics. In sum, red is scientifically proven to improve the performance of the person wearing it, intimidate competitors facing it, and create a bias among referees and judges for it. From Louis Oosthuizen's red dot on the glove, to Tiger's Sunday red shirt, to Kathy Whitworth's visualization routine, the mental game of golf never ceases to evolve.

Lastly, in today's tech-driven world, golfers ignore advanced analytics, precision measurement devices, and big data at their own peril. In the near future, the average golfer will likely have access to a system in which smart golf clubs track their swing plane, speed, and angle of attack, comparing that to the launch, shape, and distance logged by a smart golf ball and then correlate both of those with scoring results. After the round, they will sit down with their smartphone's artificial intelligence-powered golf coach app which will have crunched through their personal golf data to come up with swing change tips, course management strategy suggestions, and equipment change recommendations. The pace of adoption is breakneck in this part of the golf industry.

This book is organized starting from the short game to the long; into equipment, health, mental game, technology; and ultimately alternative ways to enjoy it. There's no obligation to proceed in sequence; readers should feel free and are encouraged to jump around. The first chapter features the evolution of putting grips because it is the clearest and most quantifiable way to show the adoption of alternative playing styles is increasing over time. The research on how green speeds have evolved throughout history in chapter two was one of the most fascinating to compile. Some of the most interesting and popular subjects, however, come toward the middle and end, such as the topics discussed in chapters four, five, and nine.

The cover of this book depicts a sequence of golf holes set on top of a box that has the illusion of always going uphill. This obviously impossible scenario was patterned after the never-ending Penrose staircase and includes surreal elements of a giant golf ball and a waterfall cascading off the side of the box. The graphic is meant to inspire us to think outside the box, to dwell on golf methods that seem impossible at first, but that might actually be groundbreaking. The greens are slanted at different angles which will become meaningful after reading chapter five. The end of each chapter includes a "bucket list" of practical ideas for implementing out-of-the-box methods. It also serves as a test to see where you fall on the spectrum of traditional vs. out-of-the-box thinking.

There were many purposes for writing this book: First, to open our minds to new ways and methods to play golf that create a paradigm shift in our pursuit to become better players, something that can be particularly encouraging and motivating for those who feel their game has plateaued or maxed out its potential. Second, to bring renewed interest, challenge, and variety to a pastime that many of us have enjoyed for decades. A wider perspective can bring into view a figurative new mountain to climb or simply an alternative way to enjoy the game in a form that hadn't previously been considered. Third, to highlight the game's increasingly strategic nature. While it's never been just about physical talent, strength, or coordination, golf has increasingly become a game of wits, the ability to out-think, out-prepare, and out-maneuver opponents before ever setting foot on the first tee. Fourth, to take readers on a journey through golf history filtered through a different lens and perspective which can instill an appreciation for its evolution and a sense of wonder for its future.

For the average golfer who has been trying to get better for years without success, perhaps it is time to think out-of-the-box, explore unconventional ways to improve as well as new ways to enjoy the game. For aspiring collegiate and professional golfers, it will be difficult to outpace the herd by following in the tired and well-trodden paths of others. From high handicap to low, every golfer can benefit from spending time out of the box.

CHAPTER 1
UNCONVENTIONAL PUTTING

The early 1960s were in many ways the glory days of golf. Arnold Palmer was The King complete with an army-sized crowd following, Gary Player was making a name for himself around the world, and a young Jack Nicklaus had just arrived on the professional scene. Television ownership was still relatively new for Americans. The percent of households with one in their living room increased from about 10% in 1950 to roughly 87% in 1960; color TVs would arrive en masse in the latter part of the decade. The frequency of professional tournament broadcasts was increasing, giving the weekend golfer visual access to their golfing heroes. For the first time, people became true fans, cheering on their favorite players, analyzing swing methods, and observing various approaches to the game.

Golf fans tuned into the old black-and-white broadcasts to find players putting in a wristy, hunched-over style,

Arnold Palmer 1964
PA Images/ Getty Images

flipping their wrists back and forth with gentle ease and freedom; Arnold Palmer and Patty Berg were chief among those using this method. Palmer often took putting advice from fellow competitor and friend, George Low, who was well known for being the center of attention and living a luxurious life on someone else's dime. Over time these attributes earned him the infamous title of "America's Guest." Aside from being one of the biggest characters and personalities of his day, he was also considered by some to be the best putter of that era. Masters champion Doug Ford reminisced in 2008 that "George Low was the greatest putter I ever saw outside of Tiger Woods, George could putt with his foot better than most guys could with their putter. That's the truth. I saw him beat a guy in Havana for $35,000 putting with his foot."[1]

George believed a putting stroke should be "wristy, but not flippy," explaining that the body should be very quiet, the only parts that should move are the arms from the elbows down. He encouraged players to hold the putter in their fingers and picture the action of a door, which hangs on and swings around a hinge – in this case your hands.[2]

This wristy style was the prevailing philosophy and practice of the day.

Patty Berg 1954
Bettmann/Getty Images

There was a beauty to the free-flowing wrists of old, a time when golfers played by feel – golf was more of an art than a science in that era. Time, however, gave way to a stroke deemed more consistent. Approximately three-quarters of tour players in the 1960s used a wristy putting style, but the popularity declined precipitously in the 1980s, and today only a handful still use the antiquated method.

Most tour pros of the modern era seek, in contrast, to lock their wrists and even arms into position to make a very methodical, controlled, pendulum-like stroke. Putting grips today are often designed with the express purpose of keeping the hands and wrists quiet. The conventional putting grip for decades had been left-hand high, right-hand low for right-handers, and a vast majority of players in the 1980s used that traditional grip. Over time players started experimenting, generally first with cross-handed grips, then long putters, and eventually the claw grip. Changes in putting styles over the decades offer the clearest and most quantifiable example of how unconventional methods are taking over the game.

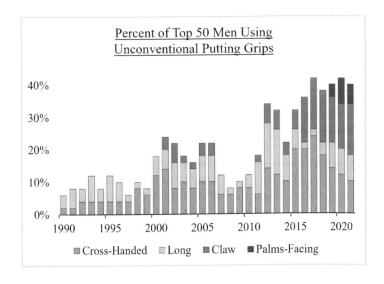

Percent of Top 50 Men Using
Unconventional Putting Grips

Cross-Handed   Long   Claw   Palms-Facing

Among the earliest professional practitioners of cross-handed putting was the 1969 US Open champion Orville Moody, although he wasn't the ideal ambassador for the unique approach. A *Sports Illustrated* article captured the sentiment of the day: "Watching him on the green is a wrenching experience. He has the air of a man facing the guillotine. He squats nervously over the ball, gripping the club cross-handed. Just before he draws the club back his right leg undergoes a series of involuntary tremors and the putter jerks. As the club comes into the ball, Moody's entire body sways forward. Some pros claim to have seen his putter stub the ground behind the ball and bounce almost completely over it. In his grip, stroke and demeanor, Moody violates every accepted rule of good putting, but it's the only way he knows... A player who putts well, it is said, can putt with anything. A bad putter tries gimmicks."[3]

In the '60s and '70s, cross-handed putting was described

as "among the more radical departures from the standard putting grip"[2], and players who ventured into obscure putting methods were viewed as bad putters simply trying to find a Band-Aid for their problem. Cross-handed putting was the butt of many jokes. Lee Trevino once remarked, "If God wanted you to putt cross-handed, he would have made your left arm longer!" Years later, another writer reflected on Moody saying, "I consider him the finest striker of the golf ball I have seen since Ben Hogan and the equal of Calvin Peete. Orville won the 1969 U.S. Open at the Woodlands outside Houston, Texas, but I truly don't know how he did it with the worst putting stroke I ever saw. It was a hybrid, a cross between a spasm and a jab that might produce a lucky putt that stopped within a few inches of the cup or leave a knee-trembler three to five feet short or long."[4]

Orville's nickname was "Sarge" because he served 14 years in the army before joining the PGA tour. He was described by fellow players like Trevino as having a big heart and by others as "golf's everyman whom we could all identify with."[5] He was always good tee to green, but his putting woes produced many lean years in the decade that followed his big win. If there was ever a US Open champion that could likewise rightfully be called a PGA tour journeyman, Orville Moody fit the description.

It took a couple more decades until cross-handed putting really started making inroads, but there were examples of success here or there along the way. In an effort to stop the bleeding from the worst part of his game, Bruce Lietzke switched to cross-handed putting in the mid-'70s which contributed to his win at the Tucson Open in 1977. In that tournament, the young and winless Lietzke was in a playoff with Gene Littler when the television commentator said he had virtually no chance of winning because he was using a "give up grip" in reference to his cross-handed technique.[6] He proceeded to drain a long putt for the win and captured three more tournament titles by the end of the decade.

Around the same time, Mike Furyk, a club pro in the Pittsburgh area, asked Gary Player and Arnold Palmer what they would change about their golf games if they could go back in time. Upon reflection, they responded it would be to putt cross-handed, remarking it was a more solid stroke. Mike passed those words of wisdom along to his son Jim Furyk and he putted cross-handed as he grew up through the junior ranks in the 1980s and into his professional career. Similarly, at the same time, Kelly Robbins had switched to cross-handed putting as a junior and took that to the LPGA tour where Jan Stephenson and Michelle Estill were converting as well.

The early '90s was the tipping point on the PGA tour, a time when players became more willing to experiment, more willing to try something new. It had been five years since Bernhard Langer won the 1985 Masters putting cross-handed and the unconventional putting party was about to get bigger joined by Fred Couples in 1992, Tom Kite in 1994, and later Vijay Singh in 1998. Thomas Bjorn also came onto the golf scene in the mid-'90s using the left-hand low method. There was now a solid group of players putting unconventionally, unlike the previous couple of decades when there were truly just one-off examples. Even with the increased popularity, it was still criticized; one news article said Fred Couples was so confused about his game that he had "resorted to cross-handed desperation putting."[6] Through the rest of the decade, however, the sharp critiques gave way to acceptance, fascination, and eventually admiration.

By the early 2000s cross-handed putting became the dominant alternative putting grip on the LPGA tour. Notable among the early adopters were top 10 ranked players at the time: Kerrie Webb, Grace Park, and Juli Inkster. The popularity of cross-handed putting on the LPGA tour has persisted to this day with nearly 20% of the top 50 using the method.

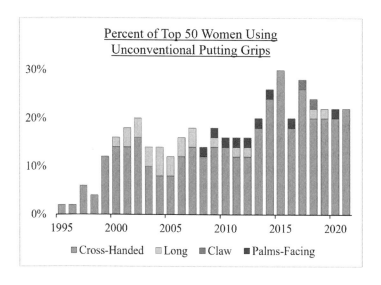

In the modern era, cross-handed adherents have included at one time or another players such as Inbee Park, Lydia Ko, Nasa Hataoka, Jordan Spieth, Rory McIlroy,

Rickie Fowler, Xander Schauffele, and many other top 50 players. This young crop of millennial-aged players is much more flexible and experimental than their predecessors. They willingly switch putting grips between tournaments depending on the greens, season-to-season depending on their performance, and for some even intra-round depending on the length of the putt. Rickie Fowler, for a time, used a conventional putting grip for long putts and cross-handed for short putts. Fowler explained that he had better feel with a conventional grip, which is why he used it for long putts where distance and lag were important. On short putts, however, making a fundamentally sound, clean stroke was more important which is what he got from cross-handed putting because it placed his shoulders into a more level position. Rickie has switched back and forth between the differing grips a multitude of times starting from his junior days and throughout his professional career highlighting the flexible nature of his generation.

Since coming on tour, Jordan Spieth has dazzled spectators with his cross-handed putting genius. Whether it was the 26-foot birdie bomb on the 16th at Chambers Bay in the US Open or the birdie-eagle-birdie-birdie finish at Royal Birkdale for The Open Championship, in the critical moments, on the biggest stages, with the most pressure, Spieth's putting seems to be unflappable. His remarkable 2017 season combined with other players such as Kevin Chappell, Pat Perez, and Billy Horschel resulted in a third of all PGA tour events being won by cross-handed putters, at least a near term culmination of success that is a far cry from the yesteryear obscurity, mockery, and ridicule of the left-hand low method.

Shifting gears to another historic trend, the story and development of the long putter ran concurrently with that of cross-handed putting. Early on, a consistent pattern emerged of players first experimenting with left-hand low for many years, then ultimately moving to long putters. Orville Moody, Bruce Lietzke, Bernhard Langer, Fred Couples, and Vijay Singh all followed this pattern, while others, such as Jim Furyk and Thomas Bjorn chose not to make the second jump.

The beginning of the long putter's story reaches back to the early '60s when Richard Parmley, an avid golfer living in Salt Lake City, was in search of a solution to his putting woes. His tee to green play was scratch-golfer quality, but the scores weren't materializing, his game being hampered by poor putting. He pondered on a way to keep his wrists unbent during the stroke and asked himself what part of the body remains the stillest – the belly was his answer! He put his research scientist brain to work and designed a club that extended to his belly. The results for himself were almost immediate and he submitted a patent application for the "Body-Pivot Golf Putter" in 1961, which was approved four years later. Parmley never did anything with his patent and Phil Rodgers was likely unaware of it when he won two times in 1966 using a long putter anchored to his belly, the earliest example of a professional using the method.

Nearly two decades would pass before long putters came back on the scene. In 1983, Charlie Owens began using his personally-created 51-inch putter anchored to his sternum on the Champions Tour, which he later used to win the Treasure Coast Classic. Orville Moody's name once again surfaced in golf history as one of the earliest adopters of the long putter. After struggling to make cuts and scratching out a living for most of his PGA tour tenure, Moody experienced a rebirth after joining the Senior Tour in 1984 and adopting a long putter which he anchored to his chest. He won three of the first five events of the season and proceeded to rack up a total of 11 wins over his senior career. He also became one of only a handful of players to win both the US Open and the US Senior Open with his 1989 win at Laurel Valley Golf Club in Pennsylvania. When asked about his new technique on the green, he said, "All I know is the putter has done wonders for me."[7]

Long and belly putters increased in popularity through the mid-to-late '80s, a trend which included players such as Johnny Miller, Peter Senior, and Sam Torrance on the PGA Tour and Jerilyn Britz on the LPGA Tour. In response to the rising, albeit still very limited, popularity of long putters, the USGA and R&A considered a rule to limit the allowable length in 1989, but ultimately decided against adoption. One of the primary reasons being the USGA's concern for players with back problems and other physical challenges that would make using a normal length putter more difficult. Additionally, restricting putter length might have been arbitrarily unfair to players of different heights. Lastly, given the very limited adoption among tour pros and amateurs alike, it wasn't seen as a widespread threat. In the late '80s, the governing bodies were more focused on the length of the putter and less so on the anchored nature of some putting strokes. A focus that would shift over time.[8]

The USGA later explained its philosophy on new trends and techniques saying, "A newly emerging method of play does not need advance approval, but rather may be used unless and until it is deemed to be in breach of the Rules of Golf. Such an approach to the Rules protects both the players and the game: it allows players to play without fear of retroactive penalties, and it allows the USGA and the R&A to study and react to an issue as time, experience, and the needs of the game permit or require."[9] Fortunately for golf, this mindset and philosophy allow for innovation and experimentation without prior approval and without trepidation for being penalized. With time, more and more players found advantages in long and anchored putting techniques.

Bruce Lietzke started using a long putter in 1990 at the Hawaiian Open. Undeterred by the jokes hurled his way, he once commented, "I putted cross-handed for 15 years before I switched, so I was used to hearing all the jokes already. You're always looking for any little edge out here. If it helps just a half a stroke per day, over four days that could turn a fourth place into a first place."[10] Lietzke applied that maverick attitude to all aspects of his life. He was probably more famous for his unique playing schedule than any of his other unconventional approaches. A natural talent, Leitzke shunned practicing and took months off at a time from golf regularly throughout the year. He tended to front-load his schedule early in the season through May and then play rarely during the summer months, even skipping the US and British Open to go on family vacations and coach his son's baseball team. His unique ordering of life priorities was often mistaken for apathy, lack of ambition, or complacency with mediocrity; some called him "America's finest recreational golfer"[11] and a "squanderer of talent".[12]

Leitzke claimed he didn't touch his clubs during the winter months. As the legendary story goes, even his long-time caddie, Al Hansen, was skeptical of this assertion; after the last event of the year he took the headcover off of Lietzke's driver and stuffed a banana inside. Three months later in February at the Bob Hope Classic, Hansen removed the cover on the practice tee to find a rotten banana that Lietzke described as being nasty, all black, and covered in fungus. The decaying produce was rancid and had ruined the wooden driver inside forcing them to throw it and the entire bag away. Not even his caddie could believe he'd go all winter without touching his clubs, but Lietzke was a family man who valued spending time with his two children and wife over chasing more money and fame. Whether it was his putting, swing, practice routine, or life in general, Leitzke couldn't care less about conventionality; he charted his own course.

In 1991, Rocco Mediate became the first person to win a PGA tour event with a long putter, capturing the Doral Ryder Open at 28 years old. On the LPGA tour, Beth Daniels switched to the long putter in early 2000 and became the first woman to win with the unconventional stick a few years later at the Canadian Women's Open. The title also distinguished Beth as the oldest winner of an

LPGA event at the age of 46, a record that still stands.

It wasn't until 2003/2004, however, when Vijay Singh won seven tournaments with the long putter, that passionate debates resumed and escalated over the next decade. There were strong opinions on both sides of the issue, even among the legends of the game, with Arnold Palmer staunchly against it while Jack Nicklaus generally struck a more neutral to accepting tone. The trend hit a tipping point in 2011/12 when, within a year timeframe, three of the four majors were captured by long-putting players: Keegan Bradley at the PGA Championship, Webb Simpson at the US Open, and Ernie Els at the British Open. It didn't take long for the USGA and R&A to jointly announce the proposal to ban anchored putting in November of 2012, officially adopting it in May of 2013, with an effective date of January 1, 2016. While the PGA tour was initially opposed to the new Rule 14-1b, it eventually reversed course and adopted it as well.

Explaining its rationale, the USGA said there were two main reasons why the previous 1989 decision was being reversed. "In contrast to the past, when anchored putting was uncommon, recent and potential future developments have brought the use of anchoring to the point where it may threaten to rival or supplant traditional non-anchored putting strokes and to alter the essential character and challenge of the game."[9] While clearly the emphasis on the importance of a free-flowing swing was central to the USGA and R&A's ruling, it's remarkable the mere fact an unconventional method was threatening "to rival or supplant" a traditional one was reason sufficient to be numbered among the points to stop its progress.

After the anchoring ban, many players abandoned long putters, opening the door and giving way to the next trend – the claw. Although there had been a small bout of popularity in the early 2000s, the claw's rise to prominence really took hold in 2015/16. It all started, however, in 1995 with Chris DiMarco who was struggling, particularly with his putter, having lost his PGA Tour card after two seasons and narrowly missed an opportunity to get it back in Q-school. He was so frustrated and downbeat that he seriously considered giving up the game, nearly resigning himself to a normal life with an ordinary job. The following year, however, Skip Kendall, a fellow mini-tour professional, showed him the claw grip while the two were killing time during a rain delay at the Disney event in

Chris DiMarco 2001
Jeff Haynes/ Getty Images

Orlando. It was a strange, unorthodox approach that Chris had never before seen, but decided to explore. There must have been some magic in the air near Disney World because the results were almost immediate and launched him into a ten-year streak that would include three

PGA tour wins, a near major championship at the Masters, two Ryder Cup appearance, $22m of career earnings, and time as a top ten ranked golfer in the world. His success could rightfully be credited to his putter as he consistently ranked among the best on tour with the flat stick. The journey wasn't without jeering and barbs from fellow players, someone dubbing it the "psycho grip" and earning DiMarco the nickname "Psycho." Throughout the years, the claw grip has been described as weird, unusual, awkward-looking, a monster, and a final act of desperation.

In hindsight, DiMarco explained that when putting with a conventional grip, his hands didn't want to work together. There was a lot of tension, and as a result, his putting stroke was short and quick. He tended to miss a lot of five to six footers. The claw grip enabled him to have softer grip pressure and a more even and fluid stroke. In the early 2000s, other top players using the grip included, at one time or another, Mark Calcavecchia, Kevin Sutherland, and Mark O'Meara, but the trend faded for a while until picking back up around 2011 with Sergio Garcia.

Sergio had always been considered one of the best ball strikers in the game, consistently ranking high in strokes gained off the tee and approach shots to the green, but if there was an Achilles heel, it was his putting, sometimes ranking as low as 168th on tour in strokes gained putting. He explained that he tended to have too much grip pressure with a traditional grip and his right hand dominated the stroke, often leading to a very controlled, mechanical motion. In January of 2011, his world golf ranking had dropped to 78th, down dramatically from the top 10 sphere where he had resided for years. During this trough in performance, Sergio switched to the claw grip which he explained took his right hand out of it and created a stroke that restored the touch and feel he had been missing. By 2013 he was ranked as one of the best putters on tour and his world golf ranking was on its way back to the top ten. In 2017, Sergio became the first player to win a major championship using the claw grip at the Masters.

In the years to come, many more players would join the claw grip club including Phil Mickelson, Justin Rose, Michelle Wie, Tony Finau, Tommy Fleetwood, Branden Grace, Louis Oosthuizen, Webb Simpson, and Kyle Stanley among others. On one of the biggest stages, in the 2018 Ryder Cup, players using the claw grip had a stellar 11-5 record.

Are these unconventional methods truly better than the traditional grip? Answering this question is a little more difficult than one might think given the players most likely to experiment with alternative putting grips are those that have already been struggling. It's not necessarily fair to compare the aggregate strokes gained putting of all claw-grip putters vs. other methods, for example, because the starting point was a group of below-average putters. Players that rank among the best in putting have very little incentive to try new methods, even if those methods might actually make them even better. A logical way to assess this is to analyze the before and after of those that did attempt a change. Looking at a representative sample of players that have changed their grips from traditional to one of the alternative methods, the median and average improvement in strokes gained putting was .22 and .31, respectively, for the three years after the change vs. the three years before the change.

While .30 improvement in strokes per round doesn't seem like a material amount at first blush, it most definitely is for tour professionals. For the average player tour, a .30 improvement per round is worth $372,000 per year, nearly $4 million over a ten-year stretch. For the top quarter of players, a .30 improvement is worth $864,000 per year. The separation between journeymen and stars is very small and any marginal improvement is worth a lot of money.

Taking a slight tangential excursion, it is counter-intuitively advantageous to be a volatile golfer, the right kind of volatile in that one has the capacity to go very deep in any given tournament – the ability to have a hot streak. The purse of professional tournaments is distributed in an exponential fashion, meaning the reward for placing in the top 30, 20, and 10 increases at larger and larger rates. Looking at money earnings and season-long total strokes gained data from 2018, one will notice a few odd data points – Bubba Watson sticking out. He earned $5.8m in official money, or roughly $241,000 per start for the year, and played .55 strokes better than the field as measured by total strokes gained. What's interesting is that there were about 20 or so other players that averaged .55 total strokes gained, but the earnings of those were $85,000 per tournament or $1.7m for the full year. In other words, Bubba Watson made about $4.1m more than he was "supposed" to have earned based on his scoring average. So what made the difference? Bubba had the ability to go low, capturing wins at the Genesis Open, WGC-Dell Technologies Match Play, and Travelers Championship, and the reward for winning is a disproportionately big check. Other professionals with a similar talent for going low and earning more than their stroke average include players such as Brooks Koepka, Justin Thomas, Hideki Matsuyama, Sergio Garcia, Kevin Kisner, Patrick Reed, and Justin Rose.

Looking forward, what the future holds for putting grips is anyone's guess. Unconventional approaches can have a short life or remain limited. Sam Snead was a pioneer of side-saddle putting, KJ Choi experimented with it for a season, and Bryson DeChambeau played a short time with it in 2017 before the USGA deemed his putter non-conforming. Mike Hulbert was likely the first person to putt one-handed during a PGA Tour event at the 1995 AT&T Pebble Beach. Years later Ian Poulter decided to putt one-handed for a few holes during the Waste Management Open. Most recently, pros have started experimenting with the palms-facing or prayer grip. As history has shown, sometimes these trends take time to develop. Chris DiMarco first started putting with the claw in 1998 and it took over 15 years before it gained wider popularity. Perhaps side-saddle, one-handed putting, or the palms grip have a future on the PGA Tour, but there's no doubt experimentation will lead to innovation, and what's considered conventional today may fade completely away like the wristy putting style of the '60s.

Turning from putting grips to putting styles, after a very difficult 2012 season Michelle Wie pioneered table-top putting in 2013 when she experimented using a wide stance, legs straight, and back bent so dramatically over from her waist that her upper body was parallel with the ground, resembling a table. At 6' 1" inch in height, Wie felt too tall and her original intention was simply to get closer to the ball. In what she described as a very natural feeling stance, she didn't realize she had descended to a 90-degree angle until people started commenting about it. Undeterred, she continued doing what felt right which resulted in dramatically improved putting statistics and a win at the US Women's Open the next year. Ignoring the potential negative impacts on most people's spines, forming a 90-degree angle has a remarkably intuitive advantage of creating a pendulum in which the clubface can

stay perfectly square through the entire stroke. For people that stand with their back at say a 45-degree angle, the mechanics of the swing necessitate the clubface slightly opening on the backswing and closing on the follow-through. This creates a

Michelle Wie 2015
Scott Halleran Getty Images

timing issue of making sure the clubface is square right at the moment of impact. With Michelle's tabletop method, the clubface theoretically could stay square during the entire stroke. For those that see Michelle's method as odd, consider, for example, how bent over Jack Nicklaus used to putt; he got pretty close to 90 degrees, albeit with an arched back instead of flat. In 2017 Michelle Wie moved away from the tabletop and onto the claw grip, closing the chapter on one of the more innovative approaches to putting the game has seen.

Pivoting to another method, conventional wisdom says that a golfer should look at the ball while putting and continue to look down until the ball falls in the cup. There's probably no better example of Jordan Spieth's maverick mentality than his method of looking at the hole when he strokes short putts rather than looking at the ball. At first, it seems so bizarre, but only a moment of contemplation gives way to the realization that in the vast majority of other sports players look at their target, not the ball. Basketball players don't line up for a free throw, then stare at their ball while shooting; bowlers don't line up for the strike, but then look at the ball; even billiard players don't stare at the white ball when going after the eight. It sounds pretty logical – look at your target.

The concept is actually not a novel one in the game of golf – back in 2008, Eric Alpenfels and Bob Christina wrote the book *Instinct Putting* in which they detailed their research on the advantages of looking at the hole while putting. Their experiments concluded that most amateur golfers would be better off looking at the hole rather than the ball for most putting lengths. While Spieth wasn't the first to putt looking at the hole nor the inventor of the concept, he certainly is the highest-profile practitioner and will likely create an entire generation of young golfers who look at the hole on short putts instead of looking at the ball.

Perhaps somewhat the reverse, but equally as unconventional, is Lexi Thompson who from time to time putts with her eyes closed. Lexi employs the technique as a means to focus on the stroke without being distracted by all the visual cues that occur in what can seem like an eternity of a simple back and forth motion. At the time she switched, Lexi said, "I basically just feel it in my stroke and take a deep breath."[13] It can be a calming technique in some of the most pressure-filled moments of golf. In addition to Lexi, other players such as Suzann Pettersen and Vijay Singh have used the closed eyes method with success.

Part of the reason why putting with your eyes shut or looking at the hole can be beneficial is explained by something called the "quiet eye" (QE) technique. Pioneering research in this field was done by Joan Vickers who demonstrated that elite golfers hold their final gaze on the ball for 2.5 - 3.0 seconds, while higher handicap golfers hold that gaze for only 1.0-1.5 seconds on average. Joan explains, "Extensive testing of golfers has shown that only highly skilled golfers are consistently able to hold the QE stable on the ball for about one second before the backswing, one second during the stroke, and a half-second after contact. Instead, for lower-skilled golfers it is more common for the gaze to shift once the stroke begins as indicated by higher fixation rates to more locations."[14] In other words, higher handicap golfers get distracted once the stroke begins; in millisecond jolts, the eyes look at the club pulling back, the grass to the side, the ball mark just in front and lose focus on the ball. Worse than that, the visual distraction opens the brain up to retrieving mental distractions, perhaps bad memories of previously missed putts or times of choking under pressure. Joan continues, "When a long duration QE is maintained on an optimal location a mental buffer or barrier is created that prevents intruding thoughts or bad experiences arising in the hippocampus and amygdala from distracting attention and leading to higher levels of anxiety." A fixed and focused gaze is a natural calming mechanism of the body and leads to better fine motor skill performance. Jack Nicklaus described this concept generally as "Concentration is a fine antidote to anxiety."

Luckily for those that fall into the non-elite golfing camp, quiet eye can be learned. In studies that included sports such as volleyball, basketball, skeet shooting, and golf, the QE-trained group improved their performance by as much as 20-30% in some cases compared to zero percent improvement in most control groups. For Jordan Spieth, perhaps focusing on the hole allows him to maintain quieter eyes than focusing on the ball. For Lexi, closing her eyes is about as close as one can get to forcing quiet eyes and eliminating the potentially fatal distractions that can occur during a stroke.

Harvey Penick's "Take dead aim" mantra shows that perhaps he intuitively knew decades beforehand the importance of what would later be proven through science and quiet eye research. In his famous Little Red Book, Penick said, "Once you address the golf ball, hitting it has got to be the most important thing in your life at that moment. Shut out all thoughts other than picking out a target and taking dead aim at it. This is a good way to calm a case of the nerves... take dead aim at a spot on the fairway or the green, refuse to allow any negative thought to enter your head, swing away. A high handicapper will be surprised at how often the mind will make the muscles hit the ball to the target... I can't say it too many times. It's the most important advice in this book. Take dead aim." Amazingly the sage advice of a teaching legend almost mirrors the exact findings of precision science decades later.

Changes in putting grips, styles, and approaches through the years offer the clearest and most quantifiable examples of how unconventional and innovative methods are taking over the game. If history is any predictor of the future, the putting styles and grips 20 years from now will be very different than those used today. Early adopters will be rewarded with a competitive advantage until the herd catches up; it will likely pay off to think out-of-the-box.

Out of the Box Bucket List:

- ☐ Use a cross-handed grip
- ☐ Use a palms facing or prayer grip
- ☐ Use a claw grip
- ☐ Use a long putter
- ☐ Try side-saddle putting
- ☐ Try one-handed putting
- ☐ Try arm-lock putting
- ☐ Putt while looking at the hole
- ☐ Putt with your eyes closed
- ☐ Putt with quiet eye technique
- ☐ Try table-top putting

CHAPTER 2
THE RACE FOR GREEN SPEED AND ALTERNATIVE CHIPPING STYLES

It could be argued one of the most consequential trends in golf history has been the move toward dramatically faster green speeds. It has impacted nearly every aspect of the game including equipment, ball construction, rules, iron play, chipping style, putting methods, course construction, and overall difficulty. Fast greens are simultaneously a rite of passage, badge of honor, and source of controversy for the best courses in the country. It all started in the 1930s with a man who, in a twist of irony, wanted to slow down what he believed were excessive green speeds.

Edward Stimpson invented the Stimpmeter in the late 1930s as a way to measure and compare green speeds. Stimpson was the captain of the Harvard golf team and won the Massachusetts State Amateur Championship in 1935. In that same year, stories from the US Open at Oakmont made headlines where none of the top 20 professionals broke 75 in the final round and Gene Sarazen putted it off the green into a bunker on one hole. Many of the pros were complaining the greens were too fast. As a result, Stimpson created a device that could measure green speeds and embarked on a journey to push its adoption which would last for more than 40 years. The Stimpmeter was at once simple and ingenious, originally a narrow wooden board about 30 inches in length with a groove down the middle. There was a small notch where the ball could be placed along the track as it rested flat on the ground on a level part of the green. One end of the Stimpmeter would slowly be raised until there was sufficient gravity for the ball to overcome the small notch and roll down the groove and onto the green. The distance the ball rolled out would be the stimp reading and showed how fast the greens were rolling. For example, a reading of ten feet would indicate a faster green than a reading of seven feet.[1]

While we can't travel back in time and test the stimp speed of historical championships, we can estimate it by watching old broadcasts and clocking the time it takes for putts to come to rest for a given length. It sounds counterintuitive at first, but putts on very fast greens will take longer to reach the hole than putts on very slow greens. Think of a 20-foot, downhill putt on a very fast green: all you have to do is tap it and the ball slowly rolls all the way down to the hole; it might take seven seconds for that putt to come to rest as it gently meanders on its way. Contrast that with a 20-foot putt on a very slow green: a solid whack is required to send the ball toward its target and after a short journey it comes to an abrupt stop on the shaggy surface; it might only take three seconds for that to occur. It becomes clear that putts on fast greens take longer to arrive at the hole than those on slow greens.

The chart below shows the evolution of green speeds in major championships over the last 70 years. The data was compiled by watching old broadcasts and clocking the time it took for a 20 foot putt to come to rest. The numbers were then converted into the approximate Stimpmeter equivalent.

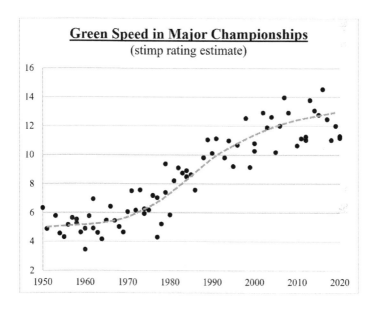

Green Speed in Major Championships
(stimp rating estimate)

While every effort was made to be exact in the hundreds of data points gathered for this study, there were natural limitations to making it perfectly accurate. Luckily, the most important and sensitive input in the calculation was easy to measure: the number of seconds it took for the ball to come to rest. Therefore, while the estimated stimp readings for each tournament might not be the exact measured result had the greens been physically tested, the big picture conclusion about how green speeds have changed over time is undiminished.

Edward Stimpson's original purpose for inventing the Stimpmeter was to rein in courses where the greens were running too fast. After watching the Masters on TV and clocking the putting statistics, Stimpson reportedly sent the Chairman of Augusta National, Hord Hardin, letters chastising him for excessive green speeds.[2] Ironically, however, it was precisely his invention and its official adoption that catalyzed the race for speed across the country.

The turning point came in the late '70s when the USGA used the Stimpmeter for the first time in a formal capacity at the 1976 US Open at the Atlanta Athletic Club; in 1978, it was officially adopted by the USGA and courses around the country started measuring their green speeds. This quantification naturally led to comparisons and no respectable course wanted to be found at the bottom of the list. The race for speed had begun and stimp readings went from an average of seven in 1978 to over ten by 1990 and have slowly crept higher ever since as advances in turf technology, irrigation, fertilization, and mowing equipment continued to improve.

Greens are becoming so fast that fans have witnessed numerous instances of balls at complete standstills being blown off the green by a strong gust of wind. For example, in 2016 Billy Horschel was analyzing a 13-foot birdie putt on the 15th hole at Augusta National when a large gust of wind pushed his ball into motion, the ball ultimately caught the false front and rolled all the way into the lake. Obviously frustrated, Billy was required to re-hit from the location of his last chip from the side of the green, but with a penalty stroke as if he had originally chipped it in the water. At the 2015 Open Championship at St. Andrews, Louis Oosthuizen was getting ready to hit a short par putt when the wind picked up and pushed his ball from a standstill to about a foot away. While Louis tried to confirm with a rules official about the next steps, the ball started moving again and ended up about five feet further away. Many players around the course were enduring similar problems. These types of situations are becoming more frequent than infamous incidents of the past such as the 1998 US Open at Olympic Club and the debacle at the 2004 US Open at Shinnecock. The need for speed is an addictive drug and has become a badge of honor for tournament hosts and golf courses alike.

Faster green speeds have also led to uncomfortable rules situations and ultimately modifications to those rules. A ball at rest on a very fast green is more easily moved by wind, natural causes, or seemingly nothing at all. For example, the rules fiasco surrounding Dustin Johnson at the 2016 US Open was the culmination of fan and player frustration with indecipherable and unintuitive rules. While preparing to make a short putt on the fifth hole on Sunday, Dustin took two practice swings next to the ball without touching it, then floated his putter at address, during which the ball moved fractionally, a dimple, maybe two. He stepped away immediately and called over a rule official who determined there was no penalty. By the time Johnson arrived on the 12th tee, the rules committee had reviewed video of the putt and reversed the on-course decision. Instead of simply telling Dustin the decision had been changed, they said it was "under review" and he *might* incur a penalty. What ensued over the next two hours was nothing less than a nuclear bomb of backlash from players, fans, and the media, including all across social media. Fellow players called the situation "amateur hour," "ridiculous," "a joke," and "laughable". The USGA reportedly received thousands of negative letters in the days after the championship, in addition to hundreds of news articles, and a plethora of social media rebukes.

It wasn't long before the USGA introduced a revised rule that stated there would be no penalty for any accidental movement of the ball on the green. Whether by wind, a steep slope, rain, or even a player's putter accidentally touching the ball, there would no longer be a penalty. This simplification was applauded as good for the game and a common-sense approach. The point here is not to beat a dead horse, revisit and rehash historical controversies, but to highlight that ever-increasing green speeds have not only driven changes in the way golf is played, but also in how it is governed. The purpose is also not to argue whether faster green speeds are good or bad for the game, but simply to analyze the impact of the trend.

From an even broader perspective, the immense impact faster greens have had on the way golf is played cannot be overstated – it has driven dramatic changes in all aspects of the game including putting grips, chipping styles, ball construction, iron play, equipment construction, course design, and overall difficulty. All else equal, a faster surface shrinks the effective target area and ability for a golfer to hold and stop shots. The exact same putt on a green mowed to a thirteen stimp will break more than one mowed to a ten stimp. In the 1960's many of the best players would take the break out of putts and ram it in the back of the cup. If they missed, the ball would only roll two to three feet by the hole. The penalty for taking the break out of a putt today might be a ten-footer on the way back in some cases. In addition to slope and speed, on a gusty day, tour players now have to take wind into account when reading a putt. If a strong breeze can blow a ball from a complete standstill off the green, it surely impacts its journey to the hole while in motion.

The rising speed of greens in the 1980s led to higher and softer chips, but most players still used a straight-back and straight-through swing path. Unconventional and innovative in his day, Phil Mickelson came on the scene with a pronounced open face, a long outside-in swing path that cut across the ball and threw it high in the air, landing softly on the ground – what is known as the "flop shot." It's not that players hadn't done something similar previously, but Phil clearly took it to another level. Phil Mickelson was born in 1970 which means he was about ten years old when green speeds increased exponentially and in the first generation that grew up on ten-plus stimp surfaces. In 1980, Phil Sr. created a backyard practice area behind their San Diego house that had a green, a bunker, and enough room to hit about a 45-yard shot. Phil has credited his stellar short game to the hours of backyard practice enabled by his dad's peculiar landscaping choice.

Phil has also been unconventional in his equipment selection, carrying at times four wedges and being among the first to use a 64-degree wedge. An earlier pioneer in the wedge arena, however, was Gene Sarazen. As the story goes, one day Sarazen went flying with business magnate Howard Hughes and noticed the wing flaps descend as they lifted off the ground. This sparked a thought in Gene's mind that affixing a flange to the bottom of a golf club could facilitate its splash through the sand, ultimately throwing the ball higher in the air. Sarazen's first homemade sand wedge had a breathtaking 50 degrees of loft, a rarity for the day, but he was proven a visionary by subsequently winning the 1932 U.S. Open and The Open Championships with his new invention. Ultimately Gene sent his homemade club to Wilson which tweaked the design and brought the modern sand wedge to the masses.

In the '60s and '70s players didn't need more than a 52 or 56-degree wedge, but increasing green speeds eventually required higher and higher lofted wedges. Short-game coach David Peltz recalled, "I built my first 60-degree lob wedge for Tom Kite in 1979. He carried it along with his sand and pitching wedges during the '80 season and quickly became regarded as one of the world's best wedge players."[3] While the new wedge was only one of many factors, Kite had only won two professional tournaments prior to 1980, but starting in '81, he won every year for the next seven. Players started using 64-degree wedges in the early 2000s with Phil being among the earliest adopters. How high lofts will ultimately go in the future is uncertain, but there's a manufacturer that has recently introduced a 73-degree wedge designed for the recreational player. As long as green speeds require it, players will seek clubs that can throw it higher and land it softer. Sarazen, Kite, and Mickelson were willing to push the bounds of conventionality in their eras, were open to thinking differently, and were all rewarded with a competitive advantage for a period of time until the crowd caught up.

In addition to wedge loft, rising green speeds in the 80s catalyzed innovations in groove technology. During that time period, Ping introduced several advances including the infamous square-grooves in the mid-'80s which enabled players to spin the ball up to 100% more than before. True sharp-edged, square-grooves only lasted for a handful of years because they chewed up the soft balata balls of the day, eventually giving way to the clubface that would last for the next several decades - the radiused U-groove. It was very similar to the square groove but slightly rounded off at the top to accommodate the balata ball while still producing a significant improvement in spin. The move to round the top of the groove famously led to a prolonged legal battle between Ping, the USGA, and the PGA tour. The USGA asserted the Ping Eye 2 grooves were too narrow after being radiused and therefore violated the rules; Ping disagreed with the measurement methodology. The PGA tour had gone a step further and tried to outright ban Ping Eye 2 clubs in 1990. A settlement was reached in 1993 and any Ping Eye 2 club manufactured before April 1, 1990, was grandfathered in for life, but going forward sharp-edged square grooves were not allowed and the radiused U-grooves had to comply with the USGA's spacing specifications.

Despite the USGA's enforcement of groove regulations in the early '90s, a fundamental shift in golf strategy was underway. A study done years later would show a decreasing correlation between driving accuracy and money earned on the PGA tour in the '90s and '00s compared to the preceding couple of decades. In other words, hitting into the rough off the tee was less penal in the '90s and '00s than it had been in previous decades due to changes in groove technology that allowed pros to produce nearly as much spin out of the rough as they did from the fairway. This gave way to the "bomb and gouge" style of play in which players crushed their drives as hard as they could with little regard for accuracy knowing they could gouge it out of the rough onto the green if needed.

The USGA conducted a wide-ranging study of the issue in 2006 and 2007 which ultimately resulted in the 2010 rules changes. The goal of the groove rule change was to restore the fundamental challenge and inherent penalties of the game. It ensured that driving accuracy was still a rewarded aspect of competition and, overall, that skill was the primary allocator of success. The 2010 rule accomplished this by limiting the sharpness of the groove's shoulders and reduced the volume of the groove's depth by about 30%, bringing the spin performance closer to the V-grooves of old.

Perhaps not directly impacted by rising green speeds but

concurrent with that trend, unconventional chipping styles have increased in popularity over the years. Most golfers are familiar with cross-handed putting, but fewer are aware of high-profile examples of cross-handed chipping. Probably the most famous golfer to cross-hand chip during competition is Vijay Singh who used the technique off and on for years dating back to his junior golfing days. In a dramatic example, Chris Couch holed out a cross-handed chip on the 18th hole during the final round of the 2006 Zurich Classic to win.

Similar to putting, using a cross-handed grip to chip levels the shoulders with the ground and creates a shallower swing path that can be more consistent and guard against chunking the ball off tight fairway lies with little grass behind or under the ball. Vijay Singh likes to use it on Bermuda grass due to the club's tendency to get caught going through impact. It works best in situations where it is not necessary to hit the ball very high or land it softly; it's best in a bump-and-run situation, the chipping stroke most similar to that of putting.

In a separate example, Jason Palmer became the first one-handed chipper on the European tour in 2015. Many years earlier during his journey through the mini-tours he caught a case of the chipping yips, a mysterious phenomenon during which even highly skilled players lose the ability to make the easiest of shots. The term "yips" was coined by Scottish golfer Tommy Armour who also described it as a "brain spasm that impairs the short game". Science has later shown people caught in this psychological trap experience involuntary muscle tremors during their golf stroke.[4]

Jason's short game deteriorated so much that he was desperate, willing to try anything. He said that every time he missed the green in regulation it resulted in a bogey, often worse. One day he was practicing with his friend Neil Chaudhuri and declared he'd had enough, that he felt his short game was diabolical. Jason then proceeded to show him he could even chip one-handed better than he was currently playing. Neil encouraged him to take his one-handed method to the course; the results for Jason were immediate and he finished second on the Alps Tour that year. He continued with the unconventional approach for several more years until 2014 when he won the Foshan

Jason Palmer 2015
Ross Kinnaird/Getty Images

Open and took second place at the Oman Golf Classic, paving the way to a spot on the European Tour. Jason didn't just use the technique around the green, he would go one-handed as far as 40 - 50 yards away. He credited the switch to one-handed chipping as having saved his career.[5] Unfortunately, an injury to his left wrist (not his chipping hand) ended up being a more formidable challenge than the chipping yips nearly a decade earlier and resulted in a premature retirement from professional golf in 2018.

What the future holds for wedge loft, groove technology, and unconventional chipping is fun to contemplate. Could we see the rise of another one-handed maverick like Jason Palmer, more cross-handed chippers like Vijay, or will ever-increasing green speeds drive players to use 70-degree wedges? As with every part of golf, the only certainty is change and the techniques used 30 years from now are likely to be dramatically different than those employed today. As has happened in the past, the true visionaries and those brave enough to adopt the unconventional will have a competitive edge for a period of time.

<u>Out of the Box Bucket List:</u>

- ☐ Carry a stimpmeter, know the green speeds
- ☐ Put a 60 degree wedge in the bag
- ☐ Put a 64+ degree wedge in the bag
- ☐ Try cross-handed chipping
- ☐ Try one-handed chipping

CHAPTER 3
FULL SWING ANOMALIES

Most golfers seek to imitate the "textbook swing", a theoretical ideal compiled from the most often used techniques of every aspect of the golf swing. For example, in the textbook swing a majority of tour players will grip the club in a certain way, a majority will have a certain position partway back, and a majority will have a particular angle at the top of the swing. In theory, the very best players in the world should be those whose swings most closely resemble this textbook ideal, but that isn't the reality that emerges when looking at history or doing a case-by-case analysis. A majority of the current top 20 players in the world break some "rule" of the textbook swing, each has an oddity, a quirk, or unique factor that makes their particular swing work. Most likely they would actually play worse if the consensus method was pursued in every single aspect. Below are a series of case-studies of some of the best players throughout history.

Arnold Palmer

There's no better place to start this discussion than with the King himself, Arnold Palmer. He was the son of a golf course greenskeeper in Pennsylvania. His swing was homegrown and homemade to match his personality – unique, aggressive, go-for-broke with a little bit of swagger, yet an unmatchable ability to relate to the masses.

Sports historian and writer Jim O'Brien once said of Palmer, "He looked like a guy who worked in a steel mill, the way he played golf, he didn't have the classic swing of Sam Sneed. He wasn't a textbook golfer, he looked like somebody who might play golf once a month on Saturday."[1] Another sportswriter observed, "His golf was flawed many times, you know he didn't have a pretty swing, he lunged at the ball. Nevertheless, it was a violent swing and that attracted you too."[2] It was that go-for-broke, aggressive nature that resulted in heroics like driving the green at the par four first hole in the 1960 US Open at Cherry Hills. He rallied from seven shots behind to be crowned champion; it always seemed to be a thriller when Palmer was in the hunt.

The most recognizable part of Arnie's swing was his signature follow-through, often described as a helicopter ending, whirly-bird, crouching corkscrew, and a twisted finish. That trademark follow-through was Arnie's way of muscling the hook out of his swing by holding it off as long as possible. As he pulled the club away from his hunched-over address, he brought it back on an inside line and bowed his wrist at the top with a closed or shut clubface, a position that otherwise would be prone to hooking the ball. Dustin Johnson, David Duval, and Graeme McDowell have all displayed similar positions and been compared to Palmer in this respect. As Arnie lunged down in an all-out attack on the ball, he had to hold the clubface off as long as possible in order to prevent the shot from going left which culminated in his iconic helicopter finish. Ever the showman, always adding suspense to the moment, he didn't let the drama stop with the whirling around. Palmer loved to coax, encourage, and even beg the ball in mid-air to go where he wanted, often leaning dramatically one way or the other. It was like so many other aspects of his game and life; it was as if he were willing the ball into the hole, an endearing trait that made it hard not to root for him.

Arnold Palmer famously said, "Swing your swing. Not some idea of a swing. Not a swing you saw on TV. Not that swing you wish you had. No, swing your swing. Capable of greatness. Prized only by you. Perfect in its imperfection. Swing your swing. I know I did." That independence of mind garnered 62 PGA tour titles and seven majors, a Hall of Fame record that makes it hard to argue he should have done anything differently.

Raymond Floyd

Raymond Floyd was born into a military family, taught to play golf by his father on the Fort Bragg golf course, and grew up to be a well-rounded athlete. He was an accomplished baseball pitcher and was even offered

$25,000 to play for the Cleveland Indians after graduating from high school, but he passed on the overture to pursue his golfing dream.

Floyd had one of the most unusual golf swings of his time and easily makes this list of highly accomplished players with unconventional swings. Bobby Clampett, who played with Floyd many times over the years, said, "Raymond Floyd was a fantastic ball striker (…) with a very unusual style of golf swing, one that was clearly his own. He didn't emulate anyone, in fact, I don't think there's been anyone that's tried to emulate Raymond Floyd's golf swing, but he's one of the greatest players of all time."[3]

From an open setup, Floyd took the club away on an inside line, rolling his wrists along the way until halfway back he had laid the club off to an extremely flat angle, the most unique aspect of his swing, a position from which many golfers would find it very difficult to consistently square the face. From there, his hands went nearly 90 degrees straight up. Sometimes he'd stop three-quarters the way back and descend from that laid-off position. Other times, he'd continue his swing to the top, rolling his wrists in reverse, back into position ultimately going from an extremely flat position to an on plane to sometimes upright one at the top of the swing. He descended into the ball in a steep manner, on a line that felt like he was slightly coming over the top and followed through to his signature finish, a three-quarter, sawed-off wrap around his body. Compared to the perfectly balanced follow-through of players like Olazabel or Hogan there was no beauty in Floyd's finish;

the club seemed to abruptly bounce off the side of his body as he leaned forward to counteract the sideways momentum.

Floyd used to take advice from golf teacher Jack Grout and once said of him, "He's the best. He doesn't teach theory or method, which is fashionable today. I don't believe in that. He takes what I've got and doesn't change anything. Some players over look [at] mechanics and fundamentals."[4] Despite his uniqueness, Floyd's Hall of Fame career credentials speak for themselves: four major championships, four senior majors, 62 tournament wins, and member of eight Ryder Cup teams.

Lee Trevino

Lee Trevino's life might be the best rags to riches story in golf, a tale worthy of an entire book itself. Born in Dallas to a family with Mexican heritage and limited resources, Trevino was raised by his mother and grew up helping his grandfather dig graves at the local cemetery. He lived in a dirt-floor shack without electricity or running water. The young Lee dropped out of school in eighth grade to work full time as a caddie at the nearby Dallas Athletic Club. It was there he learned to play golf on three short holes behind the caddie barn after a day's work carrying bags. He then went on to serve four years in the Marines, and eventually found himself back in Texas needing to support a young family. He worked various jobs including at the driving range and on a construction crew building golf courses. Additionally, he used his natural golf talent to make money on the side by gambling and hustling in head-to-head matches. By 1966 Trevino found himself dead broke and unemployed when a friend suggested he try to qualify for the US Open at The Olympic Club; he did and placed 54th, earning a windfall of $600. By 1967 Trevino was playing on tour and in 1968 he won the US Open at Oak Hill which launched him into the rest of his remarkable career.

His charismatic, outgoing, comedic personality earned him the nickname "The Merry Mex." His mouth never turned off; he was non-stop for the entire round chatting up the gallery, fellow players, caddies, marshals, and anyone else in audible range. Famous Trevino stories and quotes are too numerous to recount, but some of the most well-known are: "If you are caught in a storm and are afraid of lightning, hold up a 1-iron. Not even God can hit a 1-iron."; "I've traveled the world and been about everywhere you can imagine. There's not anything I'm scared of except my wife."; and "I'm hitting the driver so good I gotta dial the operator for long-distance after I hit it."

Just like his upbringing and personality, Trevino's swing was 100% his own, homegrown, and unique. There were skeptics early on, but their doubts soon faded. Raymond Floyd said, "When Lee came on tour, I honestly didn't think he'd make it. He couldn't hit the ball high enough to clear a one-story clubhouse. He could move the ball incredibly well, but I saw problems in-store with elevated greens and deep bunkers. Needless to say, he adapted. I was wrong."[5]

Trevino addressed the ball with his feet pointed so far left that it sometimes looked like he was aiming at a different fairway. He had a strong grip and brought the club back on an outside line with a closed face before rerouting it and dropping it back in the slot at the top. His legs were highly active, something Lee viewed as essential to his swing because he needed to clear his hips quickly and kind of squat down as the club descended. His right arm at impact was more bent at the elbow than almost any other player on tour. The combination of these moves enabled him to hit his trademark low, blocked fade. In a moment of self-analysis Trevino said, "My swing is so bad I look like a caveman killing his lunch." It certainly wasn't orthodox, but the results were consistent, repeatable, and accurate.

Jack Nicklaus once said, "I thought Trevino and Hogan were the two best ball strikers I have ever played the game with. It was a magician hitting shots. He could just do anything." Additionally, Tom Watson remarked, "You could listen to the sound of the way he hit a golf ball. The ring to that sound. Every shot. You know when someone is hitting a golf ball right. You don't have to see it, you can hear it. And Lee had that sound when he hit a golf ball."

More impressive than Trevino's unique swing, personality, or upbringing individually is the sum of it all: rags to riches, obscurity to fame, and hard work to success. Trevino once reflected, "I'm a proven fact, I'm the poster boy for it doesn't make any difference what cards you're dealt and what side of the track you come from or how far from the track you come from. If you pursue something hard enough and work at it hard enough you'll succeed." Succeed he did in so many ways, including six major championships and countless other wins around the world.

Moe Norman

Moe Norman grew up during the Great Depression in Kitchener, Ontario, Canada to a family of humble circumstances. His childhood was difficult as his unique personality, high-pitched voice, tendency toward repetition, shyness, social awkwardness, and appearance resulted in constant teasing and emotional bullying. While never diagnosed, many have since speculated that Moe had a mild form of autism that impacted him throughout his life, possibly compounded by a head injury sustained as a child. Like many from working-class circumstances, Moe was introduced to golf when he started caddying at the local golf club. He soon bought a five-iron from a member who let him pay it off at a rate of ten cents per week. His perfectionist instincts took over as he relentlessly practiced in his backyard, around the neighborhood, on close-by fields, or anywhere he could feed his insatiable desire to master his swing. Moe recalled that for over seven years, mostly as a teenager, he would hit 500-800 balls a day. Never taking a formal lesson, he grooved a motion that made sense in his mind and resulted in a remarkably consistent and straight ball flight. His family never encouraged his golfing passion; to the contrary, they often discouraged him saying he should play hockey or baseball instead. Moe's father wouldn't even let him bring his clubs in the house and he knew his father would throw them away if given the opportunity. Given this, Moe hid his clubs under the back porch, "through a little hole where he couldn't get at them because he was fat," he recalled.[6] Even in his later years, Moe said his family had never seen him hit a golf ball in real life; on TV a few times sure, but never in the flesh.

While working as a pin-setter at the local bowling alley, Norman won back-to-back Canadian Amateur Championships in 1955-56 and, as a result, was invited to play at the Masters in a letter signed by Bobby Jones himself. It's hard to separate myth from reality, but the legends of Moe at Augusta included him playing 45 holes a day during practice rounds, carrying his own bag to the dismay of Augusta membership, sleeping on course benches or in sand bunkers, hitting full practice shots off putting greens, and hitting off the first tee before the announcer had finished his introduction. The Masters had never before seen such behavior or such a character in their normally proper and formal atmosphere. While on the range one day, Sam Snead gave Moe some advice on how to hit long irons. Norman was so motivated to implement the changes that he pounded balls for the next four hours into the dark, badly damaging his hands and shortening his Augusta stay to two rounds. He returned once more to Augusta, but like so many other situations in his life, rightly or wrongly, he didn't feel comfortable or accepted there.

After turning pro, fellow tour golfers found his personality odd; he was described as a freak, clown, different, an odd duck, loner, and shy. His dress was unrefined and uncoordinated; his teeth needed an oral surgeon. He was bullied by a handful of pros at a tournament in New Orleans after which he flew back to Canada never to return to a US competition.

Like so many paradoxes that characterize the life of geniuses, Moe had a maniacal need for repetition but also went out of his way to create variety. One year he was leading the Saskatchewan Open by three strokes with a birdie putt on the last hole to win by four. Instead of extending his lead, he took out his putter and hit it in the bunker. From there he got up and down for a bogey and won by two strokes telling the crowd as he walked off the green, "Sorry, I needed the variety."[6] He said many times he would get up to a par four requiring a driver/ wedge to reach the green and for variety's sake, he'd hit his wedge first, then driver off the deck.

With time Moe's fame spread and he's often been put in the same league as the greatest ball strikers in history. Tiger Woods once said, "Only two men own their golf swings, Ben Hogan and Moe Norman," and Tiger hoped to be the third. Tom Watson likewise said of Moe, "He may be the most commanding golf striker in the game, ever." While Lee Trevino added, "I think the guy's a genius when it comes to playing the game of golf." Vijay Singh put it succinctly, once referring to Moe as "God's gift to golf."

Of all the unconventional swings cataloged in this chapter, none has been so well documented or detailed as Moe's. Hours of videos online and entire golf academies are devoted to teaching Moe's one-plane motion. Moe addressed the ball with a wide stance, a very straight/stiff left arm, his head and body leaning back, and the club resting six to twelve inches behind the ball on the ground.

His rationale for placing the clubhead so far back was that it eliminated a foot of the swing, made it very difficult to take it outside, and gave him a head start on his shoulder turn. He held the club in a two-handed, baseball-like grip that sat in the palms, not in the fingers like most golfers. Gripping the club in the palms combined with firmer grip pressure than normal was his way of keeping the wrists quiet and not too flippy. The size of the grip on his clubs was built up to a jumbo plus and his clubheads were layered in lead tape to increase the weight.

He stood far from the ball, barely able to stretch out and reach it, because that set up reduced the possible paths back to the ball. Moe took the club back perfectly on-plane in an abbreviated three-quarter wind up. As he descended toward the ball he bent his knees, squatting down through impact as his hips slid sideways toward the target, opposite the rest of the golf world which focused on a tight turn of the hips. Moe believed that while turning the hips generated a lot of power, it introduced a plethora of inconsistencies in the swing path; he was more than willing to trade distance for accuracy, once saying, "Hitting the ball pure and accurate is more rewarding than hitting it far." Moe's follow-through was held off as the clubface stayed pointed toward the target as long as possible. His finish possessed a hint of Arnold Palmer as the club recoiled and pointed toward the target in a confident pose reminiscent of Babe Ruth calling his shot. Moe said he "never let the hands get out of play," that he wanted to shake hands with the target after every swing. The result was a jaw-dropping, consistently straight shot.

Moe didn't believe in taking big divots, describing his as bacon strips, not pork chops. Often he wouldn't take any ground at all, barely brushing the grass as he picked the ball clean off the ground. When he hit driver, the tee wouldn't move as he picked it clean off its pedestal; Moe often joked he had been using the same tee for seven years. On the range, he would hit drive after drive without having to readjust the tee.

Summing up his reasoning for encouraging individualism in golf, Moe said, "Everybody is different, you can't teach two people the same. Everybody is different. Your muscles are different than mine, his muscles are different than yours… it's an individual game, every shot is individual."[7]

Moe's accomplishments were remarkable during his career – 55 Canadian tour victories, 17 holes in one, nine double eagles, three rounds of 59, and 33 course records. Moe's fame has only increased as the years have passed, amassing a huge, almost cult-like following embodying the old saying better than most; Moe truly was "the man, the myth, the legend".

Judy Rankin

Judy Rankin grew up in St. Louis, Missouri where she learned to play golf at an early age under the tutelage of her father. A natural talent, success came quickly, winning various junior tournaments including the Missouri Amateur at 14 years old. A year later she became the youngest low amateur at the US Women's Open, a record that would stand for many decades. Rankin came close to quitting golf when she was 16 after a loss in the second round of the British Ladies Amateur. Fortunately, only a couple of weeks later, Sports Illustrated called saying they wanted to put her on the cover of the upcoming US Women's Open edition, but only if she planned on playing in the tournament. With that type of opportunity, as quickly as she had quit golf, she was back in the game. Roughly one year later she turned pro at the age of 17 and started accumulating wins.

The most unorthodox part of Judy's swing was her extremely strong grip, something that was the result of trial and error experiments with her father. She discovered she could hit the ball much farther that way compared to using a conventional grip. Those experiments eventually led to Judy's dad concluding that they had found "the grip of the future." Always shorter and lighter than most of her competitors, any method that could deliver additional distance was welcomed. Harveny Penick once said, "Judy had, I believe, the strongest grip I have ever seen on a good player. Her left hand was so far over on top of the handle that she had to make an amazingly fast move with her hips to get the clubhead square at the ball."[8]

When she first arrived on the LPGA tour, there were fellow players who criticized and critiqued her grip, but Judy didn't listen and continued using what felt most comfortable. Years of success quieted the naysayers and, decades later, Judy is now revered by many as the "pioneer of the strong grip," and an example which many women golfers subsequently followed. Mickey Wright once said,

"Judy has the most unorthodox grip in golf and she has stuck with it. I admire that. She was destined to be something special. It was only a matter of time."[9]

Judy famously influenced a young Paul Azinger to continue with his strong grip. He was a teenager caddying at Bent Tree Golf Club in Florida, the location of an LPGA tournament in 1977. Paul recalled, "I saw Judy on the sixth hole during the first round, gripping that thing with a strong left hand and I just gravitated over there because I thought, 'Holy smokes, she's gripping it the way I grip it.' She shot 63 that day. I've idolized her ever since. And I never changed my grip, either."[10]

From address, she brought her swing back on a flatter plane than most players and at the top the clubface was nearly parallel with the ground, likely due to her strong grip. Using her core she powered through the downswing to arrive at a high, well-balanced finish. Rankin was known for her extreme consistency and shot-making throughout her 20+ year career.

Judy's Hall of Fame career included 26 wins on the LPGA tour before back troubles cut her playing days short. She went on to be a highly respected golf commentator and analyst for ESPN, ABC, and the Golf Channel and was captain of two Solheim Cup-winning teams.

Calvin Peete

One of the oldest adages in the game and among the first things people hear when learning to play is to "keep the left arm straight." Going back more than a century, the literature reveals golf teachers and players exhorting the necessity of this perceived basic fundamental. A *Boys' Life* article in 1930 dedicated an entire page to explaining what they titled "A Straight Left Arm Swing," saying "... let me get back to the golf swing so we can see what it is. It's entirely an arm swing, a swing back and forth with a straight left arm, the center of the swing being the left shoulder joint. Don't let anyone kid you into believing anything else." The absoluteness of this statement is striking; there was apparently no room for considering alternative methods of swinging a golf club. Boys in the '30s were advised not to let anyone trick them into believing there was another way; it was the straight left arm way or the highway. In the 1950s the great Ben Hogan said in his book that the left arm should be straight at address, on the way back, and through impact for at least a foot past the ball. A sports article written in the mid '70s asserted confidently, "The left arm *must* be straight"; another in the '80s, when commenting on the conventional thought of the day, said, "Every neophyte knows that the cardinal rule of golf is to keep the left arm straight," and another: "Even the lowliest duffer knows, one is supposed to strike the ball with the left arm straight." Similar advice was given through books, videos, articles, blogs, and other mediums in the following decades.[11,12,13]

Keeping the left arm straight has been promoted for several reasons over the years including increased power resulting from a very large swing arc and the increased ability of the body to pull the club through impact when stretched against the tension of an extended arm. Several teachers have also opined that a straight left arm enhances your capacity to hit a solid shot by keeping the distance between your body and the clubhead consistent, helping to avoid fat or thin shots. Lastly, many have argued a straight left arm reduces variability, fluctuations, and moving parts in the golf swing, boosting consistency.

Enter Calvin Peete, born in Detroit, Michigan to a large family that derived a living from the auto manufacturing industry, he was number eight of nine children. Eventually, he ended up in Florida where his dad became a vegetable picker. In his childhood, he fell from a tree and badly broke his elbow in three places; the bones healed in a fused manner making it impossible to fully straighten his left arm. After dropping out of school, Calvin worked alongside his dad in the fields eventually striking out on his own to sell clothes and jewelry from the trunk of his car in various places. Calvin didn't pick up golf until he was 23 years old but was immediately hooked and attracted to the challenge of the game. He was a natural talent and largely self-taught; he refined his game for the next decade until he made it through qualifying school to turn pro in his early 30s. Peete overcame many challenges inherent to being a black man breaking into a historically white sport and eventually became the second black player after Lee Elder to compete in the Masters.[14]

Calvin's swing was unconventional by necessity due to his childhood injury which resulted in an inability to fully straighten his left arm. He took the club away on a steep plane, almost a hint of taking it outside, while cocking the wrists back quickly. At the top, the club was pointed right of the target and his left elbow was very bent, miles away from the conventional straight position. His hips led the downswing while he squatted down, knees bent much more than normal, and body sliding forward through impact. The left arm remained bent all through impact. While very unconventional looking, Peete credits his remarkably consistent swing to good rhythm and timing. He was known as "Mr. Accuracy" and led the tour in driving accuracy for an astounding full decade through the '80s.

Peete's career record included 12 PGA tour wins, the 1985 Players Championship, two Ryder Cup appearances, and the Vardon Trophy for the lowest scoring average during the 1984 season. After his passing, Jack Nicklaus said, "Calvin Peete was a remarkable golfer; he overcame a lot of adversity, including a physical limitation, to become a very, very good golfer." He remains among the most successful African-American golfers in the history of the game.

Calvin Peete 1982
Leonardo Kamsler/ Getty Images

Nancy Lopez

Born into a Mexican-American family, Nancy Lopez grew up in Roswell, New Mexico and learned to play golf from her father Domingo, who owned a local auto repair shop. The family was of modest means, but sacrificed and invested in Nancy's golf game which produced results almost immediately. She won the New Mexico Women's Amateur Championship at the astonishing age of 12. Her high school didn't have a girls golf team, so she led the boys team to back-to-back state championships. Among many, many amateur championships and titles, she also placed second at the US Women's Open as an amateur in 1975. Like many golfers on this list, Nancy didn't have formal golf coaching or teaching aside from the occasional tutoring of her father.

Shawn Humphries once remarked, "Nancy has more moves in her swing than United Moving Company." Her response to critical comments was, "My swing is no uglier than Arnold Palmer's, and it's the same ugly swing every time." That type of wit, punctuated by an endearing smile, won the hearts of the golf world almost immediately when she burst on the scene in 1978. Her dedication to the fans, charismatic personality, and fierce competitiveness made her into what seemed like an overnight media sensation. Judy Rankins said, "There was an underlying feeling that Wonder Woman had invaded the tour."[15] One distinguishing trait was her philosophy of playing for birdie instead of playing to avoid bogey. This was evident on the greens more than anywhere else. If she missed her first putt it would often go three to five feet past the hole – she was playing to win and didn't fear the potential long par putt on the way back.

Her swing was unconventional from the beginning and the basic fundamentals didn't change dramatically over the years. At set up, Nancy stood far away from the ball, arms extended out, although still hanging down slightly. In a pre-shot move that was unique to her, right before takeaway, Nancy would lift her hands up vertically about four to five inches until the shaft and her arm made a straight line to the ball. On the backswing, she took it way inside, immediately rolling her wrists, a divergence from traditional golf teaching of keeping the wrist square for a period of time. At the top, the club crossed the line and pointed 30-40 yards right of target. From there, Nancy pulled the club through impact with her hips in a long sweeping motion. She believed a slow, smooth swing

Nancy Lopez 1979
Leonard Kamsler/Getty Images

promoted consistency and repeatable results, remarking that "the most important part of my swing is tempo, making sure when I take the club back I have good, slow tempo which helps me to finish my backswing. If I get quick, I never finish my backswing."[16]

In 1978 Nancy Lopez had one of the most

remarkable rookie seasons of any golfer in history winning nine tournaments including a stretch of five in a row and the LPGA Championship; the following year she won eight. Nancy would go on to win 48 total tournaments in her career including three major championships. Lopez was a four-time LPGA Tour Player of the Year and three-time winner of the Vare Trophy for the lowest scoring average. Inducted into the Hall of Fame in 1987, Nancy's career stands among the best in golf history.

Jim Furyk

Over the years Jim Furyk's swing has been figuratively described as "a one-armed golfer using an axe to kill a snake in a telephone booth," "an octopus falling out of a tree," "like a cowboy trying to stay on a bull for eight seconds," "a freak of nature," and "a one-man game of Twister." Even when compared to this chapter's group of unorthodox players, Furyk's swing sticks out as particularly strange.

Born in West Chester, Pennsylvania, Jim learned to play golf from his dad, Mike, who was an assistant pro at various golf clubs in the area. Mike told Jim that he couldn't play golf until he was 12 years old and the morning of his birthday Jim reminded his father of that promise, a moment that marked the beginning of a remarkable junior, college, and eventual professional career. Over the years there have been many team coaches, friends, or fellow players that have tried to "fix" Jim's swing, but he wouldn't have any of it. Mike has been Jim's only real swing coach throughout the years and both were comfortable taking an unconventional route if it meant a consistent swing and winning results.

Furyk sets up very close to the ball with his hands tight to his body. He is one of the only players to use a double overlap grip, which means that both his right pinky and ring finger are off the grip, overlapped on top of the left hand. This grip creates a more unified feel between the hands while putting more emphasis on the left hand pulling the swing through and reducing the probability of the right hand flipping the clubhead over at impact. Overall, it takes distance off the shot but increases accuracy.

As Jim takes the club away, he brings it back in a very

Jim Furyk 2019

upright and steep fashion. His hips turn less than the normal tour pro and, during certain swings, it looks as if his hips don't turn at all – a strange move that for most golfers would result in very little power. While his top-of-swing positioning has changed over the years, there was a time when his hands were up above his head with the club pointed right of the target line. From there he made his famous looping motion, dropping the club down to a flatter swing plane, turning his hips forward aggressively, with arms scrunched up against his body through impact. The result was a highly consistent fade that landed Jim among the best in driving accuracy.

Furyk has said many times that to him his swing feels straight back and straight through; it doesn't feel like it loops. Furyk has always talked about approaching the game in a natural way, once remarking, "I'm not mechanically inclined and I play the game by feel"[17] He simply swings in the way that feels natural to him and that allows him to make a repeatable motion.

Furyk won the 2003 US Open, the FedEx Cup in 2010, has 17 PGA tour wins as well as several international titles. He has played in nine Ryder Cups and holds the record for the lowest round on the PGA Tour, a scorching 58. In a testament to his consistency, he held a top ten spot in the World Golf Rankings for 15 years.

Bubba Watson

Gerry Lester Watson Jr. is better known to golf fans around the world as "Bubba," nicknamed after NFL star Bubba Smith by his dad who thought his son looked like a football player. A native of the Florida panhandle, Bubba grew up in the town of Bagdad and learned to play golf by hitting plastic balls around the house. In order to knock it further, Bubba had to swing harder, longer, and faster, but then there was the added challenge of navigating the landscaping around the house which forced him to work the ball right-to-left, left-to-right, over and under obstacles.

Thus was born the free-wheeling, swing-for-the-fences, grip-it-and-rip-it, shot-shaping style of Bubba Watson, uniquely homegrown without any input from a traditional coach or golf lesson.[18]

In more ways than can be detailed here, Bubba breaks the conventional mold as a self-described "new-age red neck." He uses a pink driver to raise money for charity, but also with the humorous, get-in-your-head purpose of taunting his fellow tour peers when he crushes it miles past them. As if a 340 yard drive can't stand on its own, Bubba highlights it in pink to make sure everyone notices. He buttons his shirt up all the way because, well, he likes it that way and plays pink, yellow, and lime green golf balls because, well, why not?

Among the earliest golfers to adopt social media, Bubba enjoys the laughs that come from his online performances. His music video on YouTube, "Oh, Oh, Oh," performed with boy band compadres Rickie Fowler, Ben Crane, and Hunter Mahan has 8m+ views and features Bubba's bare-chested dance prowess adorned solely in a pair of overalls. Also well documented online, he famously pioneered a hovercraft that has many advantages over the boring golf carts of old including the ability to drive over water hazards, through sandtraps, and over greens without damaging the course. That wasn't enough, however, and he one-upped himself by later creating a jetpack to replace the traditional golf cart. He loves to have fun and bring fun to others in the game.

Bubba's career hasn't been without controversy though. He can get emotional on the golf course in times of difficulty, openly speaks his mind, has verbally squabbled with fans, and can get testy with the media. It's just one of the many facets of the man we know as Bubba.

His style of play is self-titled "Bubba Golf," one of the key tenets being - why hit it straight when you can hit a 30-yard fade or draw? Another tenet is to swing as hard as humanly possible which is accomplished by taking the club way past parallel on an upright plane anchored by an extremely strong grip and a bent knee reminiscent of Jack Nicklaus. As he descends, the coiled power unleashes so violently that his heels come off the ground through impact, and he finishes with his hands up above his head. In an age when most are on a dogged quest for mechanical and technical swing perfection, Bubba's free-flowing, loose, shot-shaping philosophy stands out among the crowd.

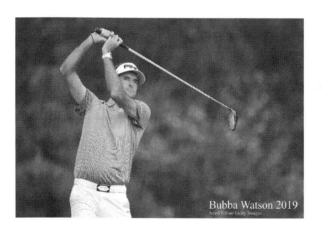

Bubba Watson 2019
Jared Tilton/Getty Images

Commenting on conventionality, Bubba once said, "When you look at the greats, no one played the same way as another or had the same teacher. You look at Palmer and

Nicklaus, they had swings that were completely different. Then you compare Seve and Tiger to those guys – completely different again. Not just the swing but how they got the ball around. Now you've got Bryson DeChambeau with his scientific approach. Commentators sometimes suggest we should play golf one way, but there are many different ways to play well."[18]

Bubba famously won the 2012 Masters in a playoff where, after driving his tee shot into the right pine brush on number ten, he bent a 164 yard gap wedge around the trees and onto the green. He would go on to win the 2014 Masters as well. Many years remain in Bubba's golf career, but his current resume includes two major championships, 12 PGA tour wins, as well as four Ryder Cup and two President Cup appearances. Bubba has consistently ranked among the top five in total driving distance on tour over the past 15 years and his world golf ranking climbed as high as number two for a period of time.

Jordan Spieth

Jordan hadn't been on tour very long before people started picking up on a unique swing aspect that has become known as his "chicken elbow" or "chicken wing". As was discussed earlier with regard to Calvin Peete, there isn't a more 101 rule of golf than "keep the left arm straight," yet Spieth willingly defies that convention. Jordan sets up to the ball with a weaker grip than normal. On the way back and particularly at the top, his left arm is very bent compared to the average tour pro and during his downswing, his knees slide forward for a period of time. Through impact Jordan's left arm continues to be bent out ahead of his body as he almost rolls onto the left side of both feet before culminating in a balanced finish.

Some have described his motion as hitting a glorified block, quirky, odd, or even dreaded. Jordan has explained he doesn't pay attention to what other people say or think about his swing, but if prodded into chicken-wing self-analysis he has remarked, "For me, it's an advantage because it holds my clubface so square through impact. The clubface doesn't rotate much, therefore, if I'm off a little bit as I'm coming down into it, it's only going to be off by a degree or two degrees versus four or five." The data backs up Jordan's assertions; while the chicken wing does result in some sacrificed distance and aesthetics, he very rarely gets himself into big trouble because the variability of his clubface is so much less than the average player. He keeps it in play and avoids the big miss.

Cameron McCormick, Jordan's long time golf coach, responds to critics by saying there are "idiosyncrasies that give the Johnny Millers of the world something to pick at and criticize," but "we've allowed [Jordan] to develop these patterns with heavy priority with what the ball's telling us in terms of function versus some architectural or appearance we want to fit into it. We've let his fingerprint be his fingerprint." He separately remarked that "It takes a brave soul to recognize that what they do is different but, yet, logic gives them the confidence to move forward and believe in it."[19]

At 27 years old, the middle and final chapters of

Jordan's career are yet to be written, but even if, for whatever reason, those turn out to be underwhelming, he has already booked major championship and PGA tour wins that are arguably worthy of a Hall of Fame appointment. As of this year Jordan has three major championships to his name, a Tour Championship, a FedEx Cup, seven other PGA tour wins, as well as three Ryder Cup and three President Cup appearances.

Brooke Henderson

Born in Ontario, Canada, Brooke Henderson grew up in a golfing family. Both of her parents were avid players, her uncle was an accomplished amateur, and her older sister played at all levels, including professionally for a time. Brooke was a natural talent, winning the 2013 Canadian Women's Amateur at the age of 15 and finishing 10th at the US Women's Open when she was 16 years old.

One of her trademarks is an explosive swing driven by an objective to crush it as hard as possible, the result of a little sibling rivalry growing up. Brooke once said of her older sister, "She's six years older than me and she was always taller, always bigger, always stronger (...) and I was always trying to still compete [with her]. I found something that worked. I found power and I knew how to get it out there just as far as her. I wasn't really thinking about it."[20]

Brooke sets up with a wider stance than normal, a foreshadowing of the power to come. Very unique to her, she grips the club about two to three inches down from the end of the club, something she has always done and a natural part of the way she golfs. At one point she tried to move her hands toward the end of the club but lost accuracy and returned back to choking down on the club. Despite being 5'4'' she uses a maximum-length driver of 48''. Particularly on her driver swing, she goes way past parallel in a very upright manner. From there she drops it down on a flatter plane, maintaining one of the most dramatic wrist hinge angles of anyone on tour. At impact, both heels are off the ground similar to the position of many long drive competitors, and she's not afraid to release the club through impact, something that requires incredible timing but offers increased distance. "I'm definitely a feel player. I think everybody is different. I know there are players out here who are extremely technical. Lots of times I don't understand what they're talking about," she once said jokingly.[21]

Brooke Henderson 2021
Julio Aguilar/Getty Images

Her sister, Brittany, said of her unorthodox approach, "She has a unique swing, but it's so athletic that you can't really mess with it too much. It's not necessarily textbook, but it works."[20] It's hard to disagree with the results – consistently ranked top ten in the world, Brooke already has nine LPGA tour wins, including the 2016 Women's PGA Championship at the age of 18, making her the youngest winner of the event. All of this was accomplished before her 23rd birthday, putting her on pace to become a Hall of Fame golfer and possibly one of the greatest women golfers to ever play the game.

Bryson DeChambeau

In many ways Bryson DeChambeau is the modern-day leader of unconventional golf thought; he's known as the "mad scientist". He possesses a characteristic trait essential to those who make breakthrough discoveries and pioneer new methods: he doesn't care what other people think. It's not that he doesn't respect and learn from other players or golf history; to the contrary, he might be the greatest golf scholar in the professional ranks. Bryson has likely read more books, analyzed more swings, experimented on more techniques, and pondered on more methods than nearly all, if not all, players in the game. He takes a very scientific approach, is maniacally detail-oriented, leverages his education in physics/knowledge of movement, and possesses a work ethic on par with past legends. Not caring what other people think in this sense means he's broken the human tendency toward conformity.

Bryson has told many stories over the years of well-meaning people who, particularly during his college days, tried to give him pointers and change his swing. While commendable in their intentions, the irony of these people approaching him on the range was their naive view that Bryson was simply unaware or hadn't been taught the correct way to swing. They were nobly going to save him from his ignorance. The reality, however, couldn't have been further from the truth; far from ignorance, Bryson was likely more knowledgeable on golf swing mechanics than the cumulative expertise of those who tried to change his methods.

For every well-meaning person, there have likely been even more ill-intentioned critics, those not so secretly hoping for his failure. Padrig Herrington summed it up well when talking about DeChambeau: "He's under a lot of pressure. There's no doubt when you do something different, everybody's watching. I won't say they're hoping you fail, but they're certainly watching and putting pressure and expectation on somebody who's out there changing things or changing the game."[93]

An overarching principle of Bryson's swing is simplification, a reduction of moving parts. The logic is intuitive – a swing designed with fewer moving parts has a lower probability of error and a higher chance of producing consistent results. He was heavily influenced by reading *The Golfing Machine*, a 1970s book that is among the most technical explorations of golf swing mechanics ever written, perfect for a physics major who also happened to be a world-class collegiate player. The book has a very appropriate word in its title: "machine". Bryson frequently references the analogy of a robot in the way he thinks about his swing, contemplating questions such as, "How would you build a robot to swing a golf club most efficiently?" Theoretical answers to those questions have informed the techniques he uses.

One major philosophy of Bryson's is to set up in an impact-like position, his hands being higher than normal and forming a straight line from the shaft all the way up his arm. Conventional wisdom is to let the arms hang straight down from the shoulders, but this creates an angle between the shaft and the arms at set up, something that is different from the impact position. Bryson's philosophy makes a lot of sense – why unnecessarily introduce more moving parts or variability in the swing? In order to achieve higher hands at address, he holds the club using an oversized grip

Bryson DeChambeau 2021

in his palms instead of his fingers like most players.

In addition to the hands being higher at set up, they are pushed forward more than normal. From a front view of his address, the shaft again creates a perfect line with his left arm, unlike most, who have a slight angle at the wrist. Overall, Bryson has created a perfectly straight pendulum from all vantage points between the shaft and his left arm. Perhaps to a greater extent than most, he begins in the position he wants to arrive in at impact.

The next major philosophy is a single-plane motion. Most golfers have multiple planes in their swing, meaning the angle of the arm and shaft during the backswing are different than the angle at set up. For Bryson, two planes in a swing is one too many when consistency is the goal. One of the main advantages of a single-plane swing is a simpler motion and fewer moving parts leading arguably to more consistent results. Part of this for Bryson includes very little wrist cock during his backswing which reduces clubface rotation, again leading to more repeatable outcomes. Through impact, his hip rotation is less than the average player and the follow-through more upright with very little torque or bend in the back.

Bryson is one of only five people in history to win both the NCAA Championship and US Amateur in the same year, putting himself in company with names like Jack Nicklaus, Phil Mickelson, Tiger Woods, and Ryan Moore. Despite that stellar amateur record, Bryson had many critics early on, but the skeptics are starting to fade as wins pile up and his world ranking resides among the elite. The adoption of new or unconventional golf swing methods happens slowly and is measured in decades. We may not know the full extent of Bryson's influence on the game for another thirty years, but we may look back at that point and view him as one of the most consequential figures in golf history.

Chapter Conclusion

While this chapter includes only a few of the many examples of unconventional swings in golf, it is hopefully a sufficiently large sampling of some of the best players of their time to demonstrate the key point: there is no uniformly-applicable, mass-teachable, textbook-ideal golf swing. Clearly, lessons can be learned from the common characteristics of great players, but one shouldn't pursue commonality in such a dogged fashion as to miss discovering a personal quirk that could open up a new world of potential and consistency. Every human body is different in proportions, strength, and flexibility. The main takeaway of this chapter is that a majority of people have an unconventional quirk that makes their personal swings work better than simply copying the textbook ideal. It's a personal key that others will have a hard time identifying and likely can only be found through experimentation and thinking out of the box.

Out of the Box Bucket List:

- ☐ Use a baseball grip
- ☐ Use very firm grip pressure
- ☐ Use an extremely strong grip
- ☐ Use a double-overlap grip
- ☐ Grip the club 2-3 inches down from the top
- ☐ Start with the clubhead a foot behind the ball
- ☐ Address the ball with a very wide stance
- ☐ Set up with an extremely open stance
- ☐ Raise your hands just before takeaway
- ☐ Use very little wrist cock
- ☐ Try a one-plane swing
- ☐ Use a ¾ swing
- ☐ Swing past parallel
- ☐ Swing with the left arm bent
- ☐ Swing as hard as possible on every shot
- ☐ Use a chicken wing at impact
- ☐ Jump off the ground at impact
- ☐ Sway your hips through impact
- ☐ Swing such that you barely take a divot
- ☐ Find a way to hold off the club through impact
- ☐ Finish with the hands pointed toward the target
- ☐ Purposely hit a 30 yard fade or draw off the tee
- ☐ Use a 48'' driver

CHAPTER 4
YOU'RE PROBABLY STANDING ON THE WRONG SIDE OF THE BALL

Golfers have likely been playing from the wrong side of the ball since the beginning of the sport. In reality, right-handed golfers should probably be swinging a club in the way we currently characterize as left-handed and vice versa. The supporting argument for this begins with a foundational understanding of handedness, as well as an appreciation for how other stick sports such as baseball, cricket, and hockey have evolved over the years. This context then sheds a new light on golf and, perhaps, flips upside down the conventional notion of how the game should be played.

First, some historical context: preference for using one hand over the other is amazingly unique to humans when compared to other species. About 90% of the world's population is right-handed with the remaining 10% being left-handed. The origin of handedness is still largely a mystery to science; some researchers claim it comes from differences in gene activity in each side of the brain, while others say that gene differences in the spinal cord are the cause.[1] Some scientists claim to have found a single gene responsible for handedness, while others say the determinant genes are spread throughout the DNA. Genetic explanations of handedness are complicated by the fact that 20–25% of identical twins (that share the exact same DNA) have opposite-handedness, one right-handed and the other left-handed.[2] This means environmental factors likely also play a meaningful role. Some experts theorize a majority of people are right-handed because the left side of the brain tends to control speech, language, and fine motor function and, in a twist of nature, the left side of a human brain also controls the right side of the body and vice-versa.

Interestingly, a majority of animal species do not show handedness and those that do are nowhere near the 90/10 split of humans. Studies of dogs and cats show almost no population-level preference for using the right or left paw; they are equally willing to claw at the door, rummage through the trash, or chew on a pillow pinned down with either paw. Collectively great apes show some hand preference; 65% of the time you'll find a chimpanzee eating figs, bananas, or leaves with their right hand, but it varies by species with gorillas and orangutans showing no dominant hand.[3] Certain types of marsupials demonstrate handedness such as the Red Kangaroo and the Red-Necked Wallaby. When needing to groom itself or eat, the Red Kangaroo tends to do it more often than not with the left hand.[4] While the scientific debate on this subject will continue on many levels, it is clear that handedness is uniquely very important to humans.

Studies show a human's dominant hand is meaningfully more coordinated than the non-dominant. A person's dominant hand is generally 7.5% stronger, can perform manual tasks about 8% faster, has a response rate 12% quicker, and is similarly more accurate in fine motor challenges.[5,6,7] These differences are consequential, particularly in a precision sport such as golf where the delineation between being a star and a journeyman is less than a stroke per round. A 10% improvement can make a world of difference; imagine hitting an average of 1.4 more fairways per round, 1.8 more greens in regulation, or being 10% closer on all chips. While it's probably not mathematically accurate to extrapolate the results of these academic experiments in a linear way to golf, the overall principle holds true – golf is a precision sport of millimeters and tiny degrees of error, even very small improvements in coordination and fine motor skills can make an enormous impact on one's score and handicap.

To up the ante, what's even more interesting are studies that show the rate of learning is also significantly better for the dominant hand than for the non-dominant. In other words, for any given task a person's dominant hand will be more effective from the start, but with repeated practice, it will also improve at a faster rate than the non-dominant hand.[7] For golfers, this means practice time and overall improvement in scoring are more productive when using the correct setup. Pulling this all together, choosing the arm/hand that will primarily control the downswing is not a trivial decision; all of this data suggests it may be one of the most consequential factors in reaching a golfer's full potential.

For most sports, it is clear which way a person should play the game. A right-handed quarterback will obviously be more accurate and effective throwing with their right arm, a left-handed basketball player will make more shots using their left, similarly with bowling, darts, water polo, handball, and dodgeball. In other sports, however, it becomes less clear which way is most effective and a variety of approaches exist. In major league baseball, if one excludes pitchers (which generally aren't on the team for their hitting abilities), 53% throw right and bat right-handed, 19% throw right but bat left-handed, 12% throw left and bat left, 1% throw left but bat right, and the remaining 15% switch hit.[8] Left-handed batting is more prominent than one might expect for several well-known reasons such as having clearer view of the ball coming into home plate when facing right-handed pitchers; a left-handed batter is closer to first base; the momentum of a left-handed swing turns the player toward first base instead of away; and the distance to the right field wall in most ballparks is shorter.

Removing those factors, it's still not clear if it's better for a right-handed person to bat on the right side of the plate or the left. On the traditional side, the left arm would lead the swing, pulling the bat through while the right arm would lag pushing the bat from behind. On the opposite side of the plate, for most people, the dominant right arm would lead, pulling the bat through while the left arm lagged. Which arm is most important? Which does most of the work, controls the path, and delivers the most power? Debate exists within the baseball community, but swing coach Charley Lau Jr. (who was A-Rod's coach for a period of time and has analyzed thousands of swings) said in his book, "What you need to remember about the hands is this: The lead-hand creates bat speed while the back-hand can slow down bat speed if it begins to dominate during the swing." He goes on to explain, "You might be wondering if the top hand has any purpose at all during the swing. It does. The top hand's primary function is to provide support for the bat through the swing, and that is an important function. You can steer a car with one hand on the wheel, but you're still better off using two for better control of the steering wheel. The top hand in a baseball swing simply provides better control of the bat. But it should never take control of the swing. If it does, bat velocity will be inhibited."[9]

It makes sense because it's easier to pull something than to push. Depending on the exact task and setup, research has shown that humans can pull about 20-50% more weight than they can push.[10] This is intuitive for anyone that has tried to move a heavy container across the floor; it's much easier to grab the handle and pull it than it is to bend over, back arched and push it. The old phrase, "like pushing on a string" has been used to describe a difficult or complex situation. Even Dwight D. Eisenhower endorsed the philosophy when he said, "Pull the string, and it will follow wherever you wish. Push it, and it will go nowhere at all."

In another demonstration of push vs. pull, if one were to place a pencil on a desk with the intent to move it in a straight line for a couple of feet, pushing it would be more difficult, take more time, and the path would inevitably be less straight than pulling it over the same distance. There's just something to this "pull is better than push" concept!

In sports, many athletic motions, such as throwing a ball, are pulling motions. When a child picks up a football or baseball for the first time, the natural tendency is to hold the ball in front of their chest and push it toward the intended target. The result is usually an immense amount of effort that ends with a weak throw traveling only a few feet. One of the first lessons kids will learn from a coach is "don't push the ball" when throwing – there is little power or accuracy in a pushing motion. The correct way to throw a football is to rotate your core backward so the shoulders are pointing toward the receiver, then the core rotates forward pulling the arm and ball, which, lagging behind, subsequently gets slingshotted through the release. Any picture of Tom Brady, Payton Manning, or Drew Brees mid-throwing motion shows the ball is still behind their helmet as their shoulders square to the target in an amazingly powerful pulling motion.

If this pulling hypothesis is correct in baseball and the lead arm controls the power and accuracy of the swing, wouldn't that suggest a baseball player should bat in such a way that their dominant arm leads? In other words, baseball players that throw, write, and eat with their right hand should really bat in the way we currently characterize as "left-handed." A study published in the New England

Journal of Medicine would appear to back up this thought process. While looking at data from 1871–2016 researchers found that those who threw right-handed but batted left were more likely to have career batting averages above .299 than any other combination of throwing and batting handedness. The success of the strategy is gaining momentum as the percentage of players that throw right but bat left has been increasing over time. What if the traditional notions of the way a right-handed person should bat were totally wrong? What if the true way a right-handed person should bat is the way we currently characterize as left-handed? It appears baseball is already on its way to making that transition.

In cricket, the most successful teams in the World Cup have nearly 50% of their players bat left-handed, far above the 24% average across all teams. Left-handed batsmen have higher batting averages, bat for longer, and are less likely to be clean bowled. While left-handed batsmen in cricket benefit from the "frequency advantage" observed in many interactive sports (opponents have less experience facing left-handers), it's possible an unattributed benefit is the fact that 51% of left-handed cricket batters are actually right-handed in every other task in their life. Perhaps a reason left-handed cricket players thrive in general is that a majority of them are swinging the bat with their dominant arm leading and thus are more accurate.[11]

Hockey is the sport most progressed in the transition to "opposite" handedness, although, as will be argued later, perhaps it's more accurate to describe hockey as furthest along in discovering correct handedness than any other sport. While roughly 90% of the world is right-handed for day-to-day tasks, roughly 2/3rds of NHL hockey players shoot left-handed, meaning the puck is on their left side, right hand high on the stick, with the left hand low. While we don't have the exact breakdown, this means that a very large portion of the NHL is playing "opposite" of traditional handedness. The number of left-hand shot hockey players in the NHL has risen over the decades from 57% in the 1920s to ~67% in present times. Additionally, that percentage is higher in the NHL than in lower hockey leagues. In other words, not only has the overall popularity of the approach increased over time, it would seem those that play with opposite-handedness have a better chance of making it to the NHL. "The Great One" himself, Wayne Gretzky, is the best example of this.

Attitudes on correct handedness have changed over time and, while a healthy amount of debate in the sport lingers, the majority of articles, videos, and youth coaches these days recommend that a right-handed person play hockey using a left-handed stick and shot. The current thought of many is that the hand placed highest on the stick controls the direction and accuracy of the shot and thus should be the dominant hand. Some argue that the right hand in hockey even drives the power if the left is simply used as a hinge on which the right hand leverages the shot.

Some countries are further along in this transition than others. In Canada, roughly 60% of youth hockey stick sales are left-handed while in the US ~60% are right-handed – seems the Americans didn't get the memo! Regardless of these small geographic differences, the big picture is that the mental transition of re-defining what correct handedness means in a stick/bat/club sport is nearly complete in hockey.

While playing opposite conventional handedness is somewhat common in baseball, cricket, and hockey, it is relatively rare in golf. In an exercise of out-of-the-box thinking, similar to concepts already discussed, why do people who use their right hand to eat, write, and throw, hit a golf ball in such a way that their left arm is the lead appendage and presumably plays the dominant role in their swing? Wouldn't it make sense for right-handed people to hit on the same side of the golf ball as Phil Mickelson? When Phil swings the club, his right arm is the lead arm and the primary appendage responsible for determining the swing path and clubhead direction. Wouldn't it make sense for right-handed people to swing a golf club in the way we currently characterize as "left-handed"?

This thesis, in large part, rests on the premise that the lead arm controls and powers the golf swing. How would we verify such a claim? One way to test the thesis is to look at players who by birth or accident are forced to play with one arm. The Society of One Armed Golfers (SOAG) was founded in 1932 in Glasgow, Scotland, an organization originally created to provide golf competitions and comradery for veterans of World War I who had lost a limb in battle. The society later expanded its reach beyond veterans to anyone who had lost the function of one arm. Annual competitions have been held almost every year since and the Society of One Armed Golfers can rightfully claim to be the oldest of its kind. A similar organization was eventually formed in the US in 1999 called the North American One Armed Golf Association (NAOAGA) that likewise holds annual championships and carries the mantra "Never Quit." The best one-armed golfers from each organization come together every two years to compete in the Fightmaster Cup, a Ryder Cup format tournament in which North America competes against Europe. The tournament was named after Don Fightmaster, a one-armed golfer from Louisville, Kentucky who was known around the world for his inspirational impact and encouragement of young men and women with disabilities to play golf.[12]

Many lessons can be learned from the players in both of these organizations. Far and away, the most important being their examples of perseverance, determination, and grit despite coping with physical limitations few are required to handle in this life. Alan Gentry, an American who lost his arm at the age of 28 in a drilling accident, said of the fellowship found at these tournaments, "It is a reason to get up every day, something to shoot for, golf was what really got me started. To say, just because I have this disability, it's not going to stop me."[13] Numerous inspiring stories are found in these organizations including literally saving people's lives. It shows the power golf has to give hope, meaning, and purpose, as well as a structure in which people can come together and form life-long friendships. These stories are reason enough to open the wallet and donate to these great organizations.

In addition to wonderful life lessons, one-armed golfers can teach us a lot about the golf swing. Some one-armed golfers choose to swing with their lead arm and others with their lag arm. Any of these golfers could turn around and do it the other way by using opposite clubs. For example, if a player's right arm is the good arm, a one-armed golfer could choose to use right-handed clubs which would require a "lag" technique or turn around and use left-handed clubs and pull the swing through in a "lead" technique. In the sport of one-armed golf, which strategy is most effective? Analyzing this question from various angles suggests a "lead" arm technique is more effective and accurate. Probably most telling, 70% of World One Armed Golf Championship winners over the last 20 years have used the lead arm technique, including the reigning champion Reinard Schuhknecht. Additionally, as

Reinard Schuhknecht 2019

Kevin Cox/Getty Images

mentioned previously, every two years the best one-armed golfers from North America and Europe come together to battle in the Fightmaster Cup, a Ryder Cup equivalent tournament. Instead of dividing up the points from matches between North America and Europe, it could also be divided up in lead vs. lag style swings. Analyzing singles match results in which a lead style golfer played against a lag style golfer, the lead style has the winning record. In the last three Fightmaster Cups, the lead arm players have a 12–8–4 win-loss-tie record in singles matches. Lastly, looking at the available data for reported handicaps of players entering one-armed competitions, the average lead arm handicap was about one point lower than the average of players with lag style swings. Obviously, exceptions to the rule exist and some amazing lag style one-armed golfers have excelled, but the rule appears to be that the lead arm does a better job controlling the swing and being accurate.

For players fortunate enough to have two good arms, wouldn't it make sense for the dominant arm to be the leading and controlling appendage given it performs functions about ten percent faster, more effectively, and with greater accuracy than non-dominant arms? A surprising number of professional golfers do, in fact, play opposite traditional handedness.

It may come as a shock to some, but Phil Mickelson, the man famously known as "lefty," is actually naturally right-handed. When Phil was learning to play golf at the wee age of two, he observed his dad's swing and sought to imitate the motion, but naturally did it in the mirror image. Phil Sr. tried to correct his son, but Phil wouldn't have it. Phil Sr. recalled, "After the third time, his swing was unlike anyone's I've ever seen for someone that young. We weren't going to fool around and change his swing. We were going to change his club."[14] Similarly, Phil's mother Mary said, "We didn't realize it at the time, and when we did, we tried to teach him to swing right-handed but it was too late. He had such a natural swing, even at that age."[15] Phil Sr. cut down the lightest set of left-handed clubs he could find and his golf career was born. In everything else, including baseball, writing, and throwing, Phil was right-handed, but golf was different.

Phil Mickelson 2015
Ezra Shaw-Getty Images

An interesting side note here is the similarity of Phil's early story with that of Tiger Woods. According to Earl Woods, a couple months shy of turning one year old Tiger picked up a plastic golf club in their garage (where he would often sit in a high chair watching Earl hit balls into a net) and his first, natural motion was to swing left-handed. He continued to swing it as such for a few weeks until, unlike Phil, he became disenchanted and switched to the other side. What astounded Earl in the moment was that just before Tiger attempted a right-handed swing with a cross-handed grip, he intuitively switched his right hand to be low. "That's when I knew he was something special," Earl would later reminisce.[16,17] While Phil's and Tiger's stories diverged, it is fascinating that the two greatest golfers of their generation both picked up a club as toddlers and instinctively swung opposite of the accepted norm.

Another prominent example is Mike Weir, who is also a natural righty that golfs left-handed, though there exists a degree of ambidextrousness in him. He considers himself right-handed even though he grew up playing hockey lefty and pitched a baseball lefty. Interestingly, Weir will serve left-handed in tennis, but play the rest of the point right-handed. He has also remarked, "Anything over-handed, I do left-handed. Like throwing a ball or serving in tennis. Otherwise, right-handed, like writing and shaving."[18] Like so many Canadians who started playing hockey before golf, their chosen side in hockey became their chosen side in golf. The young Weir at one time considered switching to be a right-handed golfer around the age of 13 and wrote Jack Nicklaus a letter asking for advice. The reply from Nicklaus was simply, "If you are a good player left-handed, don't change anything – especially if that feels natural to you." Mike heeded that counsel and has kept the letter ever since. Eventually, Mike became the first left-handed player to win the Masters, a seeming catalyst for many wins from Mickelson and Bubba Watson in the years to follow.

Before there was Phil Mickelson, Mike Weir or Nick O'Hern, however, the person who paved the path for natural righties to play left at the highest level was World Golf Hall of Fame member and New Zealand native Bob Charles. He does everything in his life righty except play, as he says, "games requiring two hands". He became the first person to win a major left-handed capturing the 1963 Open Championship in a 36 hole playoff against Phil

Rodgers at Royal Lytham & St. Annes Golf Club. He would go on to win more than 70 times around the world. Charles has explained, "I don't consider myself left-handed at all, my left side is totally useless. I wear a right-handed glove, I stand on the right side of the ball, I hit the ball on the right side of the clubface and I hit the ball to my right, whereas all you other people have a left-handed glove and you hit it to your left.

Bob Charles 1963
R&A Championships/ Getty Images

So why I'm called left-handed, I don't know."[19] Stated in such stunning simplicity, one can't help but sit in contemplative silence as a life-long paradigm and fundamental view of the world flips completely upside down.

If Bob Charles was the battle-tested pioneer, the young, up-and-comer to watch is Scotland's Bob MacIntyre, a natural righty that plays left-handed because both his parents were lefties and those were the golf clubs around their house growing up. Off to a promising start in his career, already ranked 44th in the world, only time will tell if swinging with a leading dominant arm proves to be a competitive advantage for him. While not necessarily a newcomer, Brian Harman is another notable that fits in this category. He has explained, "I was a baseball player and whenever I picked up a bat or something, I always swung it left-handed. So, my parents thought I was a lefty. But when they got me a baseball glove for my right hand, I'd catch the ball, then take my glove off and throw it back to them with my right hand. Hitting just always felt more natural from the left side."[20]

In women's golf, only one tournament has ever been won by a left-handed player, Bonnie Bryant, at the 1974 Bill Branch Classic in Ft. Myers, Florida. While lefties are still a rarity on the LPGA tour, the numbers are inching up through the ranks of women's golf including on the Symetra Tour. Brittany Benvenuto, who won the 2008 Pennsylvania State Women's Amateur and played for the University of Arizona, is a natural righty that plays left-handed. Additionally, Erica Shepherd who won the 2017 US Girls Junior Championship and currently plays for Duke is a lefty golfer of unconventional handedness. When she was a toddler, her father put a bucket of balls between Erica and her brother Matt. He was hitting right-handed so she naturally went to the other side of the bucket, started hitting lefty and never changed.[21]

More common than the previous examples are natural lefties that play righty. The list is shockingly impressive, some among the best ball strikers in history – Ben Hogan, Arnold Palmer, Moe Norman, JoAnne Carner, Carol Mann, Nick Price, Curtis Strange, Johnny Miller, Blaine McCallister, Ayako Okamoto, Henrick Stenson, Christie Kerr, Georgia Hall, and Jordan Spieth among many others; all of them left-handed in most life tasks, but currently play or played golf right-handed. A major reason for this was obviously equipment availability; it was simply difficult to find quality lefty clubs for several decades. Nick Price explained a story all too familiar in this regard: "The strange thing is that I am actually left-handed in any other two-handed game, but when I started playing golf we had but one left-handed club." Additionally, a cultural bias against lefties discouraged it for many decades; there was an era in which it was common for school teachers to use a ruler to slap the wrist of any child trying to write with their "wrong hand." In the golf world, Harry Vardon (part of the "Great Triumvirate" that dominated golf from the 1890s through the 1910s) was once asked who was the best left-handed player in golf, to which he responded, "Never saw one worth a damn."[22] The 1947 Open Champion Fred Daly, a Northern Irish golfer, famously remarked about lefties, "I don't teach deformed golfers."[23]

Ben Hogan has long been regarded as among the very best golf strikers in history; his golf book *Five Lessons* is one of the best-selling of all time and players down through the generations have studied and sought to replicate his fluid motion. In it, Hogan said, "I was born left-handed – that was the normal way for me to do things. I was switched over to doing things right-handed when I was a boy but I started golf as a left-hander because the first club I ever came into possession of, an old five-iron, was a left-handed stick. I stopped being a left-handed golfer for what might be termed local commercial conditions: the boys in my hometown, Fort Worth, used to buy our golf clubs (at a dollar per club) at a five-and-dime store, and there simply never was any left-handed equipment in the barrel where the clubs were stacked. When I changed over to the right side, possibly as a hangover from my left-handed start I first used a cross-hand grip." Close friends of Hogan also appear to have confirmed at one time or another his left-handedness, but it's worth noting that there is a little bit of controversy due to a later interview in which he appeared to contradict himself on the topic. While acknowledging a couple of conflicting sources, what Hogan put down himself in black and white ink in his best-selling book is probably the most reliable source. A remarkable fact about a legend of the game.

Among the best women golfers of all time and one of the earliest examples of opposite-handedness was Hall of Famer JoAnne Carner, endearingly nicknamed "The Great Gundy" and "Big Momma." She was a fierce competitor but also known for her welcoming and tutoring care of new players on the LPGA tour. She was often found chatting up the gallery and wasn't afraid to show her passion for the game on the course. Carner was the first person to win three different USGA Championships – the US Women's Junior ('56), Amateur ('57,'60,'62,'66,'68), and Open ('71,'76). That combined with 40+ victories on the LPGA tour ranks her among the top ten women players in history, all accomplished playing opposite of convention.

Another early example is Carol Mann, who ranks 12th on the all-time LPGA tour win list with a total of 38, including two majors. She started playing golf at the age of nine as a way to get closer to her father who loved the game. Carol's father traveled often and when he was back in town, he would play golf with his friends. Learning how to play meant getting to spend more time with her dad.

While she was naturally left-handed, he made sure that she did not have left-handed clubs, adamant she used right-handed ones.[24] She played that way for the rest of her career, something that was possibly a huge benefit.

On the other side of the world, Ayako Okamoto was originally a star left-handed pitcher for the 1971 Japanese national championship softball team. She eventually grew tired of softball and at 22 years old picked up golf. While naturally left-handed she started golfing right-handed and never looked back. Leveraging incredible natural athletic talent, within a few years she was playing golf

Ayako Okamoto 1987
Focus on Sport/ Getty Images

professionally and went on to win 62 times internationally, 17 of them on the LPGA tour. She was a superstar in Japan; Juli Inkster once said she went out to dinner with Ayako while in Japan and it was like being out to dinner with Michael Jackson or Michael Jordan. As one of the first successful Japanese golfers on a worldwide stage she was a national hero and loved by the population generally.[25]

Woven throughout many of these stories is a philosophy of the lead arm dominating and controlling the swing. The only reason Moe Norman played golf right-handed was because the first club he ever owned was a five-iron bought during his caddie days from a member. Moe often talked about the importance of the left side in his golf swing once saying, "I'm pulling so hard [with the left side], this [right hand] is doing nothing. My left hand is pulling like mad. My right hand is only going along for the ride." The importance of a left-side driven, pulling swing is a theme also promoted by Greg Norman. The Shark was ranked number one in the world for 331 weeks, the longest streak in history second only to Tiger Woods, and is reportedly yet another example of unconventional handedness. Norman consistently emphasized the importance of his left side controlling the swing. He explained, "I was more of a left-side player, just power through the left side. I always had my calluses on my left hand but never had calluses on my right hand. Because my right hand just went for a ride. If my right hand started dominating which it couldn't because of my grip, you'd get in this flippy motion and my left hand was really my driver."[26] His left hand and arm controlled the swing in a pull motion, arguably a major factor in his driving consistency and iron play. Lastly, on this point, Johnny Miller would often practice one-armed shots explaining, "The thing that set my swing apart probably the most was that I was the first guy to have an early-set, and I got that from hitting balls one-handed. When you hit balls one-handed left-handed, you always set the club gradually. By halfway up, you're already at 90 degrees with the forearm and so you don't have to do anything until you're way down here and then release it." [27]

When Henrik Stenson was asked if he ever considered playing left-handed he frankly replied no; it was a very easy decision because as a kid he always played hockey right-handed and that carried over to golf. He has cited players like Phil as support for his choice to golf opposite tradition.[28] Funny enough, however, when the European Tour had a playful left-handed nearest-to-the-pin challenge during a 2017 practice round, Stenson won, despite prefacing his shot by saying, "Let's see how rubbish I am left-handed, I know I ain't good." He then proceeded to stick it two feet from the pin from 120 yards out!

A more recent example in women's golf is Christie Kerr who is also a natural lefty that was convinced by her father at a young age to play golf right-handed in order to have access to better coaches that were accustomed to helping righty players. She has 20 wins on the LPGA tour including two major championships.

Last but not least on this list is Jordan Spieth. On Jordan's 20th birthday, his mom shared with golf fans a list of 20 things people might not know about him. Among learning things like Jordan's love for country music, Texas sports, and fishing, fans also learned Jordan was an accomplished left-handed pitcher growing up, played basketball left-handed, but golfed righty. Obviously, the left arm has an unusually important role in Jordan's swing as discussed earlier with what many term his chicken wing. One of the reasons he has less dispersion is precisely because he pulls the club through impact in an extended fashion with his left arm which keeps the clubface square to the target for longer. This is accomplished in an overly pronounced pulling motion.

Some may be reading this book thinking there's no way to change after decades of swinging a certain way, even if it's not ideal. Perhaps the takeaway from this chapter is an increased awareness of the need to let the lead arm take control of the swing regardless of whether that happens to be your dominant arm or not. Byron Nelson once said, "Whatever you do, make sure your left hand dominates your right from the time you take hold of the club until you finish the swing. If you hold the club with the same pressure in each hand, your naturally stronger right hand will overpower your left hand and take control of the swing, with disastrous results."[29] Byron promoted the idea of applying more grip pressure in the left hand to emphasize its influence and control of the swing. Some players seem to take this approach to an extreme; Fred Couples' right hand nearly lets go of the club through impact, the grip pressure is so light in that hand. Likewise, Kathy Whitworth, who holds the record for most LPGA Tour wins in history, was a strong advocate of the left side dominating the swing as the only way to optimize power and accuracy. Overall, the ever-mounting evidence for a golf swing founded on a pulling motion is hard to argue against.

For those courageous enough to switch to the other side and spend a couple of seasons relearning the game, more than ample evidence exists from other sports, from golf itself – and greats, like Mickelson, Carner, Speith, Palmer, Kerr, and Hogan – to suggest it would be worth the sacrifice for the prospect of achieving one's full potential as a golfer. It's certainly out of the box!

Out of the Box Bucket List:

☐ Experiment golfing opposite conventional handedness

CHAPTER 5
HORSES FOR COURSES AND THE RISE
OF THE SWITCH HITTING GOLFER

The term "horses for courses" comes from the racing world where it is widely believed that certain racehorses perform better on specific racetracks. Every racetrack is unique with varying chute configurations, turn sizes, straight distances, shapes, dirt compositions, average air temperatures, and finish line locations. When that variation is overlaid with the physical variation of the horses themselves, it makes sense that a specific course might be more suitable to certain horses than others.

Similarly, the layouts of certain golf courses are better suited, in some cases, for right-handed players and, in other cases, for left-handed players. The differences arise from the unique shot shape, controllability, and miss dispersion of each side. A majority of golf analysts and professional golfers agree that a fade is easier to control than a draw. A fade is created by delivering the clubface slightly open at impact relative to the path, a motion that results in the clubface pointing toward the target for longer than a draw swing, which Phil Mickelson describes as requiring a skilled ability to time the release. Additionally, a fade generally flies higher with more spin, landing softer than a draw which commonly flies lower with less spin and runs out after it hits the ground. For this reason, Lee Trevino has jokingly said, "You can talk to a fade, but a draw won't listen!" When speaking of this comparison, Nick Faldo stated that it's "just a little easier to block and hit a power fade than to turn it over and hit a draw."[1] Similarly, Phil confirmed, "it is so much easier to hit a big rounded cut than it is to flip a hook," when talking about tee shots that require accuracy.[2] This means dog-leg right holes are generally easier off the tee for right-handers and vice versa.

The more important difference, however, comes in the dispersion pattern of approach shots. A missed shot that's blocked will generally travel a shorter distance than a normal shot, while a pulled shot will travel a longer distance. This creates unique dispersion patterns for right-handers vs. left as pictured on the following page. The data displayed is the nine iron dispersion of the author. Professional golfers would have a tighter dispersion both in distance and miss, while high handicappers a wider one. In both cases the angled nature would remain.

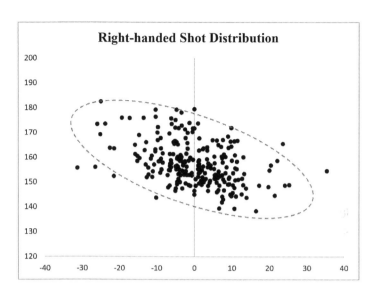

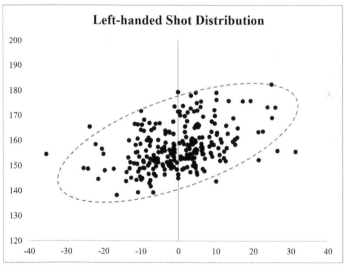

For approach shots into the green where the combination of distance and aim is critical, this natural shot dispersion has meaningful implications. Greens that angle up to the left and down to the right are easier for right-handers because a slightly blocked shot could still find the front of the green and a pulled shot has a chance of landing on the back. The opposite is true for left-handers making greens like number 12 at Augusta much easier to hit than for right-handers. Phil Mickelson has described it this way, "I think holes like 12, which is a very difficult par three, sit perfectly along a left-handed shot dispersion, short left, long right, so you aim at the middle of the green and you have a huge green to hit at. It's the opposite of a right-handed shot dispersion. You aim at the middle of the green, you pull it, it goes long left, you push it, it goes short right into the water."[3]

Jordan Spieth similarly talked about the 12th: "I see an extremely well-designed par three. It's a lot better design for a left-hander than a right-hander because the left half of the green is at a shorter distance than the right half. So when we pull the ball right-handed, the ball goes further. When we push a ball, it goes shorter. Lefties are the opposite... For a right-hander, you got to hit a really good shot. The reason it's so tough is because there are swirling winds and the green depth is so small."[4]

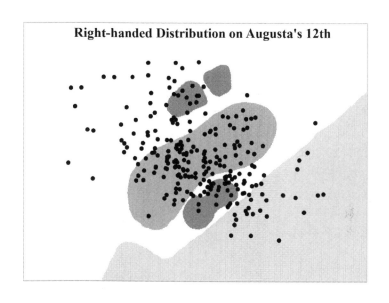

Right-handed Distribution on Augusta's 12th

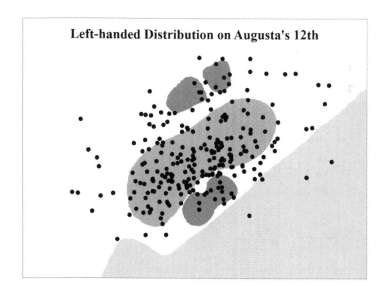

Left-handed Distribution on Augusta's 12th

This difference can have tournament-determining consequences. How many right-handed golfers have slightly blocked a shot on the short par three during critical parts of the tournament? In the final two groups of the 2019 Masters, four out of six players found the water at the 12th. Tiger Woods, who avoided the hazard, would go on to win by one shot. If those unfortunate golfers had been playing left-handed, a slightly blocked shot of the same magnitude would likely have found the front of the 12th green, but because they were playing right-handed it meant the exact same miss had the higher penalty of finding the water. Now this situation reverses itself on Augusta's par three 16th where the green angles the other way. Phil Mickelson has said the 16th is a difficult tee shot because if he comes out of it a little, the shot will go short left into the lake, but if he pulls it, the shot will end up far right on the top shelf of the green and is a possible three-putt bogey.

Overall it is well known that Augusta National favors left-handed players with 6 out of the last 18 winners being left-handed, about 33%, which is obviously well above the percent of left-handers entering the tournament of less than 5% for any given year. Numerous players have talked about the advantages of being a lefty at Augusta, but how could this be quantified? Isolating it precisely can be a challenging endeavor given the number of variables in play, but looking at it from several angles reveals some interesting insights.

First, players entering the Masters are of varying skill levels which can be represented by their average total strokes gained for the season (or season scoring average for data pre 2003). For example, over Phil's career at Augusta, he entered the tournament with a total strokes gained advantage over the average competitor of about .87. In other words, if Augusta were just like every other course on tour, Mickelson would have similarly beat the field by roughly .87 strokes per round in the Masters over the past 25 years. The reality, however, is that Phil beat the field by an average of 2.14 strokes, the difference of 1.27 being in large part attributed to the favorable setup for left-handers. Running this same analysis for other lefties (with enough rounds at Augusta to make the data meaningful) shows an average of .94 strokes of outperformance relative to expectations. That's pretty remarkable, nearly a full shot per round, or a total of four strokes over the course of the tournament.

Outperformance of Expectations by Left Handers at Augusta
Strokes per round relative to the field

Phil Mickelson	1.27	
Steve Flesch	1.28	
Mike Weir	0.66	
Bubba Watson	0.54	
Lefty Advantage	**0.94**	**Strokes Per Round**

A second method is to simply look at the scoring average of all left-handers playing in the Masters of 73.35 and compare that to the long term average of all players at 74.16, a difference of .81 strokes. While the data is not perfectly apples to apples as there wasn't always a lefty in the field each year, it does provide another finger in the wind and directional indicator. A pattern starts to emerge: holes 2, 3, 4, 8, 10, 12, and 13 are the prime spots where the lefty advantage manifests itself.

	Hole by Hole Scoring Average at Augusta		
	Long Term Averages		
Hole	**Lefty Golfers**	**All Golfers**	**Lefty Advantage**
1	4.25	4.24	-0.01
2	4.75	4.79	0.04
3	3.96	4.08	0.12
4	3.23	3.29	0.06
5	4.23	4.27	0.04
6	3.15	3.14	-0.01
7	4.20	4.15	-0.05
8	4.76	4.83	0.07
9	4.15	4.15	0.00
10	4.22	4.31	0.09
11	4.40	4.29	-0.11
12	3.17	3.28	0.11
13	4.52	4.79	0.27
14	4.14	4.18	0.04
15	4.73	4.78	0.05
16	3.15	3.15	0.00
17	4.17	4.16	-0.01
18	4.18	4.23	0.05
Total	**73.35**	**74.16**	**0.81**

The last method is to compare Tiger Woods and Phil Mickelson, the best righty and lefty golfers of their era. This comparison is intriguing because they have eight green jackets between the two of them and numerous rounds while playing at the top of their respective games; both players are long off the tee and have fantastic short games. Heading into the Masters tournament over this 25-

year span, Tiger was a better golfer than Phil by .81 strokes per round on average when playing normal courses on tour (any comparison to Tiger is brutal, even for Phil). During the Masters, however, their scoring average in head-to-head showdowns was almost identical at just under 71. The conclusion being that Phil was able to pick up about .80 strokes per round on Tiger at the Masters due to the favorable course set up for lefties.

Tiger vs. Phil at Augusta			
1995 - 2020			

Hole	Tiger	Phil	Lefty Advantage
1	4.18	4.20	-0.02
2	4.65	4.56	0.09
3	3.88	3.78	0.09
4	3.19	3.14	0.06
5	4.18	4.16	0.02
6	3.00	3.17	-0.17
7	3.95	3.95	0.00
8	4.67	4.59	0.08
9	3.97	4.03	-0.07
10	4.14	4.13	0.01
11	4.17	4.26	-0.09
12	3.19	3.10	0.09
13	4.39	4.24	0.15
14	4.03	4.05	-0.01
15	4.41	4.51	-0.10
16	2.93	3.10	-0.17
17	4.03	3.98	0.06
18	3.99	4.01	-0.02
Total	**70.95**	**70.97**	**-0.01**

Tiger's Strokes Gained Avg vs. Phil	0.81
Lefty Advantage at Augusta	**0.80**

Looking at the hole-by-hole differences in scoring reveals a fascinating pattern. The holes favoring Phil generally have greens that angle from bottom left to top right and/or dog-leg left. Holes such as 13, 12, 2, 3, 8, 4, and 17 all have these themes. Where Tiger gains strokes back from Phil are opposite in nature, generally greens angling from bottom right to top left and/or dog-leg right. These would be, most notably, 16, 6, 15, 11, and 9.

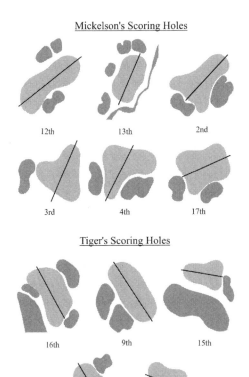

Mickelson's Scoring Holes

12th   13th   2nd

3rd   4th   17th

Tiger's Scoring Holes

16th   9th   15th

11th   6th

All this evidence shows that there are undoubtedly "horses for courses" in golf, certain layouts tend to favor particular types of golfers. In baseball, batters face a similar "horses for courses" scenario. It's easier for right-handed batters to face left-handed pitchers and vice versa because facing an opposite-handed pitcher gives the batter a clearer and longer view of the ball coming into home plate. The way some baseball players capitalize on this variation is to develop the ability to switch hit and turn the circumstances presented to them to their advantage. Some of the most famous switch hitters include Mickey Mantle, Chipper Jones, Eddie Murray, and Pete Rose.

Pat Venditte took this concept to the mound as an ambidextrous switch pitcher with the ability to pitch right-handed or left-handed. As a boy, his father trained him to throw a baseball with both hands and kick a football with both feet. When facing batters, Venditte pitches with the hand that gives him, as the pitcher, the advantage. This not only includes the batter's handedness but wind conditions and ballpark setup as some stadiums have different lengths to each respective outfield wall. Not only does Venditte benefit from the optics of the ball coming into home plate in the way he wants, but he also gets less tired during a game because he uses two arms instead of one. He plays with a six-fingered glove with two thumb slots which allows it to be seamlessly interchanged between hands during the game.

Chaos famously broke loose at the Yankees' minor league game when Venditte faced a switch-hitting batter during which, before the pitch, both sides continued to switch back and forth. The game came to a standstill as the refs tried to figure out what to do in a situation that had no rule to govern it. Shortly after the MLB issued the Pat Venditte Rule which states the pitcher must first choose which side to pitch from during an at bat, then the batter can choose the side from which he wants to bat. While the rule somewhat eroded Venditte's advantage against switch hitters, he maintained it for everyone who can't switch hit. After years in the minors, Pat got called up and made his MLB debut with the Oakland A's in 2015.

In cricket, a growing group of batsmen have shown the ability to successfully switch sides just before the ball is delivered by the bowler. Kevin Pietersen, the flamboyant South African who ultimately played for England, is credited as having pioneered this move in a test match against Sri Lanka in 2006. He was the most prolific user of the switch hit in the years to come, many times in critical moments.

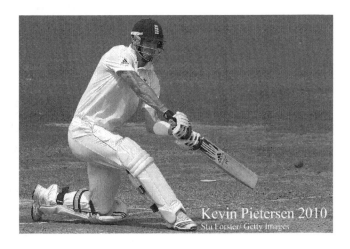

Kevin Pietersen 2010
Stu Forster/Getty Images

It generated a lot of controversy at the time with critics saying it gave batsmen an unfair advantage over bowlers. Proponents of it argue switch hitting is a very difficult maneuver, requiring a significant amount of skill, and adds excitement to the game. A batsmen with the talent to switch hit mid-bowl can exploit gaps created when the other team sets up the field wrongly assuming the batsman will hit a certain way. It also catches bowlers off guard and alters the strategy for a bowler thereafter. After years of debate, the International Cricket Council ruled switch hitting as acceptable in 2012. Pietersen is now retired and ranked on some lists as among the top 50 cricket players of all time, clearly a pioneer of cricket strategy.

If baseball and cricket players can successfully develop the ability to switch hit or pitch at the highest levels of their game, why couldn't golfers do something similar and turn the varying scenarios encountered on a golf course to their benefit and competitive advantage? It's not as outlandish as some might initially think, particularly as hitting left-handed for fun has become somewhat of a fad on social media recently for a handful of golf pros. It all seemed to start during a 2017 Scottish Open practice round in which the European tour had a "left-handed challenge" on one of the par threes as a fun and entertaining side competition. These tour pros, with no practice whatsoever, got up on the tee and attempted a 118 yard shot left-handed into the green. While fans certainly witnessed a few bad shots, it was remarkable how many players just stood up there and stuck it close to the pin; Henrik Stenson put it within two feet... and that's with no practice!

It has also become a fad on social media for righty golfers to post their lefty golfing abilities. In 2017 Jason Day posted a video of himself crushing a lefty drive 285 yards. A couple of years later Brooks Koepka posted a video of himself hitting a 293 yard lefty drive with a swing that looked like he'd been doing it that way for years. Not to be outdone, Dustin Johnson joined the party and posted a 311 yard drive lefty. Around the same time, Rickie Fowler and Justin Thomas live-Instagrammed an 18 hole match playing lefty against each other. While their lefty swings are obviously unrefined in their current states, these short snippets demonstrate an enormous amount of potential and capacity.

A golfer bold enough to train from both sides to a point of being equally skilled would be rewarded with the capacity to bend probabilities in their favor unlike any other golfer on the course. Every tee and iron shot situation could be matched up with the ideal shot distribution, increasing the probability of success and decreasing potential pitfalls. Looking back at the data from Tiger and Phil, while the lefty advantage at Augusta is roughly .80 strokes per round, the theoretical advantage for a golfer that could switch hit with equal skill could capture as much as a 1.30 stroke per round advantage over the field, a stunning 5.2 strategic stroke advantage for the entire tournament before even teeing it up. In order to develop this type of talent, one would likely have to start from a young age, practicing switch hitting for years. Perhaps, however, a current pro courageous and ambitious enough to try it would be Bryson DeChambeau. Just as he became a long drive phenom in a matter of months, let's suppose one of these years Bryson surprises the golf world by cultivating switch-hitting capacity over a winter and debuting it at the Masters. The back nine strategy could look something like the following sequence:

Bryson steps to the tee on number 10, a dogleg left down the hill which favors a left-handed drive and a soft fade. In the middle of the 10th fairway, he analyzes the green noticing a bunker off to the lower right side of the green, exactly where a blocked shot from a right-handed player would land. Instead, he pulls out his left-handed eight-iron and sticks it on the green. On the 11th tee, he pulls out his right-handed driver and hits a baby fade lined up with the shape of the hole. In the middle of the fairway, he notices the green slants up to the left and down to the right with a lake on the left side, a shape that highly favors a right-handed shot distribution; a fact he had also confirmed by the statistics which he reviewed before the round. Unfortunately, he slightly blocks the shot but luckily the ball lands short right, safely on the fairway in front of the green. A similar shot left-handed would have found the water. The famous par three 12th is well-known to favor a left-handed shot distribution, so Bryson grabs his lefty pitching wedge. He pulls it slightly, but it safely lands on the back right side of the green. The same miss right-handed would be in the trees over the left side of the green. The par five 13th hole calls for a lefty drive faded around the bend and similarly the approach heavily favors a lefty iron. Bryson knows the stats, 13 is the number one rated hole for lefties and a place he can gain ground on the right-handed portion of the field. Fast forward to the 16th hole over the water, green angled back left to front right, a perfect distribution for a right-handed swing. The approach on 17 would be a lefty wedge, while the drive on the 18th a righty driver. For an equally skilled player from both sides, matching the shot situation with the shot distribution dramatically increases the probability of a good score. By thinking out of the box, Bryson gave himself a statistical 5.2 shot edge on the vast majority of the field across the full tournament in this hypothetical scenario.

While it may seem fanatical now, the logic underpinning the advantage of a switch-hitting golfer is rock solid. The theory, however, doesn't stop with shot dispersion angles. A hole, that is otherwise neutral in setup, could call for a right or left-handed shot depending on pin placement. A location tucked tight right just over a bunker would be better attacked with a right-handed fade, while a pin tucked left would be better targeted with a left-handed fade. This point is amplified by the previous discussion of increasing green speeds. It is obviously possible to attempt these shots with a draw, but increasingly hard and fast greens make it that much more difficult to hold a generally lower height and lower spin draw on the green. A similar argument could be made when trying to hold a shot up against the wind.

Other situational benefits could include how to approach varying topographies and terrains. Golfers know that hitting a clean shot with the ball below their feet is harder than on a hill where the ball is above their feet. With the ball below, the hosel is at risk of hitting the ground first, twisting the head, and sending the ball in the wrong direction. All else equal, a switch-hitting golfer could change every lie to position the ball above the feet, increasing the probability of a clean hit.

One of the biggest pushbacks to switch hitting is the incorrect perception that stocking a bag with seven right-handed clubs and seven left-handed clubs would deteriorate the scoring of both methods, thus nullifying any theoretical benefit to switch hitting. A major trend already underway in the golfing world, however, is precisely toward using fewer clubs or what some term a minimalist set. The rationale, aside from carrying a lighter bag and introducing more creativity into the game, is that scoring doesn't deteriorate with fewer clubs. Anecdotal evidence fills golf message boards and blogs; a few of these minimalist advocates have even put it to a more rigorous test. Ed Mate, executive director of the Colorado Golf Association, is a big proponent of fewer clubs in the bag as a way to encourage growth and enjoyability in the game. He has a plan dubbed "Five-Club Golf" in which a player needs a club to tee off, a couple of irons for the fairway, a wedge, and a putter. A low-single-digit handicap golfer, Ed experimented over a 15-year span playing, at times, with as few as six clubs and as many as 14. His handicap hovered around two regardless of how many clubs were in the bag. Ed ultimately concluded that the law of diminishing returns starts around eight to nine clubs for the vast majority of golfers, particularly higher handicappers. The marginal benefit of the ninth through fourteenth club is minimal.[5]

Another example is Christopher Smith who set the

world record for speedgolf in 2005 at Jackson Park Golf Course in Chicago, shooting a 65 in 44:06 minutes while using only six clubs. In speedgolf, the score and time are added together making the official Guinness world record 109:06. Smith would argue that the rushed pace of play actually helps scoring by eliminating many of the mental game distractions and traps that often plague slow-playing traditional golfers. While the decision to put six clubs in play was likely primarily designed to lighten the load while running, it obviously didn't create a drag on scoring. Adding to the credibility, Christopher's world record performance wasn't a fluke as he has since posted many rounds in the 60s while playing with only a handful of clubs in the bag. These examples should make a switch-hitting bag setup split evenly between righty and lefty clubs at least plausible to the initially skeptical mind.

In professional tournament play, switch hitting has surfaced in small ways over the years, mostly in the putting category. The most famous example is Notah Begay who won four tournaments while putting from both sides of the ball using a double-sided putter. While at Stanford, his coach came into possession of a study done by two San Jose State basketball players and avid golfers, Tim Holman and Ed Stack. The research demonstrated the benefits of switch putting depending on the break. Golfers have always known sliders are difficult to make, putts that slope left-to-right for right-handed players. Statistically, players make fewer sliders than opposite breaking putts because of the tendency to under-read the break, leave the face open at impact, and swing on an inside-out line resulting in a lip-out at the bottom of the cup. Notah was so convinced by the study that he switch hit for the rest of his college career and on to tour.[6]

Blaine McCallister was a switch hitter in the sense that he was righty for everything in golf except putting, which he did left-handed. Growing up Blaine dreamed of playing baseball in the major leagues and was a switch hitter at the plate, something that made it more natural to carry the concept over to golf. He putted left-handed because it felt natural and he was more consistent.[7] In another example, when lefty-swinging Nick O'Hern's putting started to deteriorate toward the end of his career he switched to right-handed at the suggestion of his coach. Nick ended up having Ping make him a double-sided putter which he used left-handed for putts outside 15 feet, where distance was more important, and right-handed inside 15 feet where he found he was more accurate on the opposite side.

Perhaps switch hitting through the entire bag is a bit aggressive for some so a baby step in this direction would be to carry one opposite-handed sand wedge. This could be advantageous in numerous circumstances. For example, a ball landing in a greenside bunker could come to rest nestled up against a steep left lip requiring a very awkward, sometimes impossible stance. A switch-hitting golfer, however, would simply pull out their left-handed sand wedge, assume a very natural, level stance on the other side of the ball and dramatically increase the odds of saving par. Similarly, sometimes a ball stops just to the side of a trap requiring players to take a stance in the sand while hitting a ball that's out of it. A switch-hitting golfer would just turn around and hit from level ground. The advantages aren't limited to just sand traps; when hitting a chip from a steep hill, it is often easier to make good contact with a ball above the feet than trying to lean way over when the ball is significantly below one's feet.

For lower handicappers, an approach shot of 30-60 yards to a pin tucked into either corner of the green demands a high and soft shot with lots of spin. Generally, to hit a higher than normal sand wedge, players open the face slightly and cut across the ball which also produces some sidespin. For a right-handed player, this means the ball will spin a few feet to the right after hitting the green. This becomes problematic if the pin one is trying to access is tucked in the left side of a green. To get it close, a right-hander has to take the more precarious route of aiming straight at or slightly left of the hole. A switch-hitting golfer, however, would just pull out the left-handed sand wedge, aim a few yards right of the stick and let the natural side-spin created from cutting across the ball spin it toward the hole after hitting the green.

For higher handicappers, an opposite-handed club could be a useful "get-out-of-trouble" club. For those that spend time in the high fescue or native grass, the ball comes to rest in unpredictable lies. Sometimes a tuft of grass just behind the ball impedes the swing path, a killer in certain circumstances. A switch-hitting golfer may find, however, that by simply turning around, the swing path is clear. There could be a big difference between being able to move the ball 100 yards down the fairway vs. having to chip out sideways.

Some might advocate simply taking a right-handed sand wedge, flipping it upside down and swinging left-handed when an opposite swing is required. While some highly skilled players have become proficient at this shot, it is much more difficult than doing it with an actual left-handed club. Using a club flipped upside down requires perfect timing and pinch of the ball. Anything else runs the risk of chunking or blading it.

For golfers unwilling to switch hit to any degree, the lessons from this chapter are still valuable. When faced with a green positioned opposite a natural shot dispersion shape, there's value in being honest about the situation at hand. In low probability scenarios, such as the 12th green at Augusta for right-handers, the objective might change from hitting it close to simply hitting it on the green. Knowing that the average score for right-handers, even for Tiger Woods, is well above par can change the strategy and ultimately the outcome. Every time a player gets a par on Augusta's 12th, they've gained nearly a third of a stroke on the field.

Golf is a game of probabilities and ideally players will set themselves up with the highest likelihood for success on each shot. Sometimes the highest probability choice is unconventional or unintuitive. Bryson DeChambeau has talked about the concept of playing golf like a casino, his oft-quoted saying of "I'm trying to be the house" is simply another way of saying he's trying to set up the law of averages in his favor. That doesn't mean every shot goes his way or he wins every tournament, but if he sets up the probabilities in his favor, all he has to do is play enough times and the numbers inevitably bend in his direction and the wins start to accumulate.

Earlier in the chapter, the potential hole-level benefit of switch hitting was theoretically quantified as 1.30 strokes per round, but the incremental potential benefits of shot-level situations discussed subsequently could push that number even higher. It's not unreasonable to believe a switch-hitting golfer could capture a 1.5 stroke per round advantage over the competition, a full six shots per tournament! For context, to be a top ten player on tour, a person needs to score 1.25 strokes better per round than the average player. The edge created by hitting both lefty and righty could vault an average tour player to one of the best in the game. Switch hitting is possibly the biggest game-changing move available in golf today and would likely be a durable competitive advantage for decades, as many will be unwilling to invest the time and energy necessary.

It's a statistically similar decision to what NFL coaches face on fourth down. A vast majority of teams choose to punt on fourth down, a consensus move which initially seems like the smart decision with a single down remaining. Over the last 15 years or so, however, numerous studies have quantitatively demonstrated that NFL coaches should be "going for it" on fourth down much more often than the current tendency. Every location on the football field can be associated with a statistical probability of scoring points or an expected value. An unemotional and completely rational coach would only make decisions that maximize the probability of scoring, but in real game situations, coaches are still more conservative today than the numbers would recommend. It's a head-scratcher that an entire group of highly experienced and intelligent coaches has been getting it wrong for so many decades. Then again, humans are naturally emotional about decisions and risk averse, particularly in situations requiring a divergence from the masses.

Among the first to go rogue in this respect was high school football coach Kevin Kelly who heads up the Pulaski Academy Bruins in Arkansas. He never punts on fourth down no matter the location on the field, always goes for two points after a touchdown, and always attempts an onside kick. The strategy was formed, in part, after reading an academic research paper on the subject and seeing it as both a way to gain an edge on the competition and make up for the generally smaller-sized players at his school. His approach drives competitors crazy who, for the most part, still use the old-school mentality of punting. The results are incontestable with the Pulaski Bruins winning six out of the last seven Arkansas State 5A Championships. Inspired by this and other examples of success at various levels of football, NFL coaches as a whole have increasingly been going for it.

In many situations, embedded biases can be tempered by understanding base rates such as the fourth down example just given, but what about situations in which no historical data exists to analyze? What if, for example, the NFL had a rule for 25 years that teams were required to punt on fourth down - it was mandatory? Let's suppose at some point the NFL decided to change the rule and allow teams to go for it. How would coaches know what to do without any historical context? NFL statistics nerds would be at a loss with few numbers to crunch. The only answer would be experimentation, trial and error, a willingness to be different. The early adopters of going for it on fourth down would be rewarded with a huge advantage until, slowly, the competition would come around to the same conclusion.

Similarly, with the concept of switch hitting in golf – there is no historical precedent, few numbers to crunch, nor examples to follow. A solid theory with reasonable logical backing makes it compelling, but it requires players who are willing to experiment, perform trial and error, and be pioneers. The feasibility of learning to switch hit mid-career has been demonstrated by professional baseball players such as Ji-Man Choi and cricket players such as Kevin Pietersen. These examples should make it at least plausible a tour pro could do the same. In all likelihood, a successful, professional-caliber switch-hitting golfer will emerge having trained as such from a young age. Even if that is the path, today's ten year old junior golfer could be on tour in ten short years. If the thesis is proven correct, the early adopters of switch hitting will be rewarded with an immense advantage, likely for a long period of time, until the competition arrives at the same conclusion and catches up.

Out of the Box Bucket List:

- ☐ Try switching hitting through the full bag
- ☐ Carry one opposite handed wedge
- ☐ Try switch putting with a double faced putter
- ☐ Putt opposite the rest of your bag

CHAPTER 6
UNCOMMON TOOLS OF THE TRADE

Humans tend to externalize failures and golfers are no exception to this mentality. "I would have played better if these clubs weren't pieces of junk!" might come from the disgruntled weekend player as their bag flies through the air into the greenside lake. While it's easy to dismiss these episodes, there might be more truth in the outbursts than first thought. The reality is equipment does matter and quite possibly could be a major reason some golfers aren't achieving their full potential. The clubs, grips, and training aids golfers use are the tools of their trade and for a person with a hammer, every problem looks like a nail. There is, however, an increasingly diverse set of tools from which to choose, many have low adoption rates now but could become the norm in 10-20 years.

Currently, the most notable and talked about unconventional approach to equipment is the single-length iron set, a trend being driven by Bryson DeChambeau.

Understanding, however, the history of traditional variable-length irons is an important foundation. What we know about early golf club construction comes primarily from the antique sets that have been preserved and passed down over hundreds of years as well as from historic paintings. The Troon Clubs are considered to be the oldest existing golf set in the world, consisting of six woods and two irons, originating from Scotland and currently on display in the British Museum of Golf. They are generally dated anywhere from the early 1600s to mid-1700s and are stamped with the letters JC, initials believed to be of the owner, not the clubmaker. Notable for this discussion, the oldest clubs in existence were all of varying lengths. In a separate example, another of the oldest golf sets in existence went up for auction in London in 2012. Built by Scottish settlers in New Zealand, the set clearly shows varying lengths of clubs with the larger-headed clubs longer than the smaller-headed clubs. Finding full sets of 200-300 year old clubs is difficult, often antique clubs are collector's items sold one at a time or as a collection of mismatched clubs.

Luckily, a meaningful number of historical paintings offer a pretty clear view regarding this question over time. A mid-1700s painting of golfers at St. Andrews by an unknown artist depicts four men of obvious social status playing golf accompanied by two caddies holding, curled under their arms, a set of six to seven clubs of clearly varying lengths. Dated 1847, Charles Lees' painting *A Grand Match Played Over St. Andrews Links* is considered the most famous golf painting in the world and currently hangs in the National Portrait Gallery of Scotland in Edinburgh. It depicts a suspenseful two-man team match between Major Hugh Lyon Mayfair and John Campbell on one side and Sir David Baird and Sir Ralph Anstruther on the other. There was a large crowd gathered around the green as onlookers leaned in to see what must have been a critical putt in the match. Prominent in the foreground are the two caddies, one holding a set of clubs under his arm and the other over his shoulder. The clubs are clearly shown to be of varying lengths and sizes. Lastly, *The Drive* by Charles Brock, dated in the late 1800s, again shows differing length clubs. By the early 1900s, golf club sets became more standardized, increasingly mass-produced, and inching ever closer to the gradually increasing lengths with which the modern player is accustomed.

The conclusion of this short walk through history is that, since the very beginning, clubs were built with varying lengths. The main reason this was done was likely the same as today and centered on the desire for increased distance. When considering the tradeoff between distance and accuracy with regard to club length, the earliest golfers opted to favor distance. This made a lot of sense back in the day because pin-point accuracy wasn't rewarded or demanded to the same extent in centuries past as it is on modern golf courses. The same types of paintings referenced earlier give us a view into early golf course architecture. Courses in the 1700s and 1800s were generally links-style, very natural in state, void of trees, and set over largely unaltered rolling hills. While there existed something that resembled fairways, they were still very rugged; a bad lie in the middle of the fairway must have been very common. Compare that to the modern golf course – often tree-lined, immaculate and smooth fairways, with thick rough. Today green complexes commonly have steeply undulating topography, thick rough, deep sand traps, hard/fast greens, and pins tucked tight to trouble. The reward for accuracy on approach shots specifically has clearly increased over the centuries and decades. Even golf courses that have remained largely unchanged for the last 100 years require more accuracy solely due to increased green speeds which have shrunk the effective landing zones on approach shots.

While clubhead and face technology have clearly advanced over the decades, the basic length and lie angle of the modern golf set hasn't changed much over the past 50 years. Club sets generally start around 36" and increase in half-inch increments. Along the way, the lie angle and clubhead weight slowly decrease to account for the longer and heavier shaft. These three variables have to be coordinated in such a way to produce even gapping in shot distance. There's a lot of complexity in that optimization.

William Ockham was an English friar and philosopher of the 12th century credited with the term later known as Ockham's razor, a line of reasoning that essentially states "the simplest solution is likely the right one." Williams's verbatim phrasing was "entities are not to be multiplied without necessity," and subsequent philosophers have reinforced the belief stating, "It is vain to do with more what can be done with fewer." Recently the theory has been widely applied in business and science. In the investment industry, firms have found that financial projection models with the fewest lines of code and inputs are generally more accurate in their predictions than algorithms with more lines and complexity. In manufacturing, the trend towards simplification is promoted through lean manufacturing, Ockham's razor regularly cited as a supporting principle. Modern scientists frequently use it to assess two competing hypotheses on a given subject or event. While not full proof in its application, Ockham's razor is regarded as a sound guiding principle and sanity-check in many pursuits of knowledge.

Enter the concept of the single-length iron, arguably the Ockham's razor for golf equipment, a simpler, more elegant approach to playing the game. The argument for increased consistency is quite logical – with all the irons the same length, golfers reduce the variability in how they swing. For a stock shot of any given iron, the ball placement, swing plane, and swing speed can be nearly identical and, therefore, likely more repeatable when using clubs of the same length compared to clubs with differing lengths and lie angles. Bryson DeChambeau explains, "The one-length iron philosophy works for me because it allows me to have the same golf swing no matter what the situation out there whether it's from the rough, a sidehill lie, anything. I'm hitting the same exact type of shot, swinging the same exact way. That ultimately decreases the variables that I have allowing me to hit the ball more consistently."[1]

The concept of single-length clubs is not new. Bobby Jones was rumored to have used a version of single-length irons and looking at old photos of the clubs in his bag, it appears correct. Moe Normon, widely regarded as one of the best ball strikers ever, used single-length clubs. Noting these few exceptions, the trend never caught on broadly in the professional or amateur spheres of the past. Tommy Armour Golf introduced a set of single-length irons in 1989 but had limited adoption as some golfers complained about inconsistent distance gapping between clubs. In the decades to follow, other niche manufacturers also offered various versions of single-length sets, but again the approach never caught hold. For decades the philosophy lacked a high profile believer and example of success.

Fast forward to Bryson DeChambeau who, at the suggestion of his golf coach Mike Schy, read *The Golfing Machine,* a book that promotes a one-plane swing methodology. It's a highly technical and mathematical book that suited his analytical mind perfectly. Bryson discovered, however, a one-plane swing was difficult to implement using clubs of different lengths. In order to accomplish it, he was required to alter his posture and swing plane angle for each iron. Bryson then asked his golf coach, Mike Schy, what he thought about the concept of a single-length set. The two worked together for several nights in a row to build a set of single-length irons by cutting down an old Ping set, taking metal out of certain heads, and adding lead tape to others in a quest for same-length clubs that were likewise equal in weight. They were quite ugly, mangled, and old according to Bryson, but it gave him a test set to implement his idea.

The two went out to DragonFly Golf Club and Bryson

had 160 yards in on the first hole, par four. He took out his eight-iron and the ball landed just like he would expect. The second hole, par three, was 205 yards and Bryson turned to his coach saying, "This is going to be the kicker." He hit the ball and, despite using a five-iron significantly shorter than conventional length, it flew all 205 yards. After that shot, he turned to his coach and said, "This could be a game-changer!"[2] With time, Bryson's confidence in his idea has strengthened and he now opines it's a movement that "will literally revolutionize the golf industry."[3]

The naysayers' biggest worry is lost distance, but the physics major in Bryson explains that weight is added to low-lofted clubs such that the total mass remains the same and, therefore, the lost distance is actually minimal to none at all. Even if there were a modest loss in swing speed, the key question, however, is whether the extra distance of variable-length irons is enough to compensate for the associated inaccuracy. The consensus of players adopting single-length iron sets is no. As discussed earlier, the nature of the approach shot has changed over the centuries and decades. Whereas golfers used to hit across links-style, tree-less, gently rolling hills, today's golfer regularly faces the need to stick an iron shot onto a postage stamp green running 13 on the stimpmeter to a pin tucked tight behind a bunker. For approach shots specifically, the value of accuracy in the equation has increased.

The argument for single-length clubs is so simple and compelling, it's hard to imagine adoption won't significantly increase from here. In 30 years variable length irons might be a thing found only in history books, going the way of feather balls, persimmon woods, and hickory shafts. Playing single-length irons is probably the easiest unconventional method to adopt and capitalize upon in the game today.

Changing topics from club length to the number and types of clubs in the bag. Among the earliest records of commoners playing golf was an account in 1604 of six boys caught skipping church meetings on the Sabbath to play at North Inch, Perth. Based on other records, it's very likely they were playing with three to six clubs, a number that would rise dramatically as the game increased in popularity. Analyzing old golf paintings, videos, and pictures, we can piece together a visual of the average number of clubs used over the centuries and decades. From the mid-1700s to mid-1800's golfers generally used five to seven clubs carried in the bare hands or under the arm of a caddie. Starting in the latter portion of the 1800s some forward-thinking golfers figured they could gain an advantage by carrying more options. At the turn of the century, the average number of clubs carried was getting as high as ten and caddies could no longer handle the bare-handed carrying method, giving way to the golf bag. Among the first appearances of a golf bag in paintings and pictures came around 1890.

By the 1930s players willing to break the mold in a meaningful way believed they were finding advantages over the field by adhering to the more-is-better philosophy. Partially driven by the approval of steel shafts in 1929, players were split on which shaft to use; the easy answer for some was to simply carry both. The average number of clubs in use by the mid-1930s was around 18 when the USGA surveyed the US Open field, but Bobby Jones carried as many as 25 during some rounds, similar for Walter Hagan. The highest recorded total in the 1935 US Open was 32 clubs, carried by a player who had a full set of lefty and righty clubs believing he didn't want to be disadvantaged at any distance if his ball came to rest on the wrong side of a tree. Lawson Little, one of the best golfers of the 1930s, is credited with pushing the governing bodies to the brink by winning four majors in two years, the British and US Amateurs in both 1934 and 1935, using a set of clubs that by some accounts numbered nearly 30 in total including six different types of wedges. Shortly thereafter the USGA and R&A announced the 14-club limit rule that took effect in 1938.[4,5]

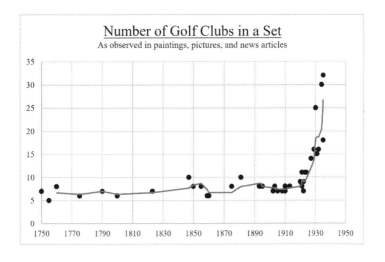

Today players are limited in their number of clubs, but they can think out of the box on what mix to carry. Phil Mickelson has probably been the most creative in his club selection lineup over the years, matching the sticks he puts in the bag with the course he's going to play. It ranges from putting two drivers in the bag to completely taking them out. When using two drivers, Phil has recently deployed a 10.5 degree to hit "cute little fades" in the fairway and 9.0 degree in order to hit "high, nasty bombs." Conversely, his strategy in the 2017 Open Championship at Royal Birkdale was to go driverless in order to combat the extremely narrow fairways. For irons, Phil has deployed up to four different models at the same time. For three iron through five iron he has played a variety of cavity-backed Callaway irons, most likely for some extra forgiveness on longer shots. Then from the six iron distances on down, he uses a muscle-back/blade iron model likely for increased shot control. Known for his flop shot magic, Phil has carried as many as five wedges at a time and was the first player on tour to use a 64-degree wedge with regularity. Lastly, lead tape is frequently adhered to the back of his clubs, even to his putter, as he optimizes mass across his set. Overall, the number and variety of club combinations Phil has used over the years are hard to completely catalog, but he clearly hasn't been afraid to experiment. He is the original mad scientist on tour.

Analyzing the clubsets of tournament winners over the last decade reveals several interesting trends. The most prominent is the move toward more wedges in the bag and higher lofts. Around 2010, tour pros carried an average of

3.1 wedges including their pitching wedge, but by 2020 that number had risen to nearly four wedges. In order to make room for an additional wedge, most players have been sacrificing one of their long irons, usually the three iron. In 2010 roughly 70% of winners on tour had a three iron in the bag, but in 2020, that dropped to under 30%. The most common wedge lineup in 2020 was PW-52-56-60, but you have players like Phil Mickelson, Dustin Johnson, and Bubba Watson who often carry a 63 or 64 degree. The adoption cycle of an additional wedge happened over a short period of about ten years, much faster than many of the other trends discussed in this book. In 2020 the best players in the world nearly universally agreed that carrying four wedges resulted in better scores than three, but in 2010 a player showing up to a tournament with four wedges would have been considered an outlier, unconventional, or unorthodox. For a period of time, those players willing to be different and forward-thinking had an equipment selection advantage until the herd caught up and the edge went away.

A slower adoption timeline occurred with the 60-degree wedge, first used by Tom Kite in 1980. He later reminisced, "Well, I was the first one to go to the 60-degree wedge way back in 1980. I don't want to say it revolutionized, but it certainly changed the game. I put it in the bag and I instantly became a better player. I didn't know anything about clubs, except I knew what I needed in terms of loft and length to get the ball to go the distance that I wanted it to go. So I put that in the bag in June of 1980, and in 1981 I was the leading money winner. I didn't finish out of the top ten for years... When I stuck it in, it was weird. It was cutting edge. Some people were anxious to see what happened, and other people were saying, 'Ah, this is the stupidest idea ever.'"[6] From there, the percentage of tour players using 60-degree wedges increased slowly through the decades, eventually passing ~70% in 2010 and hitting ~90% in 2020. It is somewhat incredible that there existed a competitive advantage, open for all to see, a new tool eventually proven to lead to better scores, and it took a huge portion of professionals four decades to adopt. In the modern era, Phil Mickelson was the first to use a 64-degree wedge regularly starting in 2006 and there has since been a slow crawl of other players putting it in their bag. What if, however, history is about to repeat itself as it did with the 56 degree and 60-degree wedges of the past? It's not inconceivable that in 2046, four decades after Phil debuted it at Winged Foot, there will be a 64-degree wedge in every tour player's bag and one will be able to look back and ask the question of why others didn't adopt it more quickly. This could fit hand-in-hand with the trend toward bulking up and hitting it longer. Who needs a three or four iron when you can hit a five iron 235 yards? It seems logical to allocate those spots to a couple of extra wedges.

Moving to unconventional grips, a trend that has swept through golf over the last decade has been that of fat-gripped putters. Like so many other developments in putting, the objective of fat-gripped putters is to silence the hands. Using a traditional-sized grip leaves the clubface exposed to small movements and twists in the hands while a larger grip makes that more difficult. With the hands somewhat disabled, the putting stroke becomes more pendulum-like, driven by large muscles, and delivers a more consistent clubface at impact. Lastly, larger grips make some of the newer grip styles easier to execute, particularly claw-style approaches.

It all started when K.J. Choi watched an infomercial for fat grips in 2006. He later said, "When I first got it, it was ugly, it was big. I didn't want to – but I practiced with it and it actually felt good. So I kept with it, but I was too, you know, I wasn't sure if I could just bring it out on TOUR. I was very hesitant because it was so big and ugly. But I kind of gathered the courage to bring it out here and for me, it's all about business here."[7] Shortly thereafter he won the AT&T in 2007 and The Players Championship a few years later. As is often the case, wider usage took many years. Jason Dufner used it at the 2011 PGA Championship where he placed second, something that gave the grip a lot of TV publicity. By 2012/13, players were increasingly using the fat grip including a new PGA tour rookie with lights-out putting named Jordan Spieth. Depending on how one defines fat putter grips, roughly 35-40% of winners on the tour in recent years have used a larger than normal grip, up from being nearly non-existent 15 years earlier.

While abnormally fat grips haven't made their way to irons and drivers in a big way yet, Bryson DeChambeau makes a pretty compelling case for a trend in that direction: "If you were to think about it. In any other sport, there is not as small of a grip as [in] the game of golf – baseball, tennis. They are able to swing it at 90 miles per hour, but what it allows them to do, especially for a tennis player, it allows them to control the face a little bit more. It's a fine-tuned skill to be able to control where the face is going in tennis, but they are able to swing it just as fast with a bigger grip." As an amateur in 2011, Bryson tested out JumboMax grips which are significantly larger than normal and found a meaningful improvement in his shot dispersion and ability to control the clubface. He's explained, "What this [large grip] allows me to do is control the face on another level. The reason is because there is more surface area touching my hands. When there is more surface area touching my hands, there is more neurological input to my brain. I have a better understanding of where the face is because I'm holding more of the club. If it's just in the fingers, it's a very small and dull representation of where the face is."[8]

A nascent movement is building in the game of golf toward less moving parts in the swing. As discussed earlier, putting was a very wristy endeavor in the 1960s, but modern players strive to do the exact opposite by reducing hand and wrist action as much as possible. For many players the full swing continues to have a very pronounced wrist cock, mostly because that allows for greater distance as the club gets pulled and released through impact. As players have become stronger over time, the need for a pronounced wrist cock might be diminishing as is the case with DeChambeau's swing. If that trend continues across golf, the adoption of grips two to three times the current size for irons and woods might help keep the hands and wrists quieter during a full swing and provide greater clubface control as is the case with putting. Imagine a fat putter grip on an iron or driver. It would look pretty ridiculous in today's world, but there's a reasonable case in 15 years or so it could become the norm as has happened with putting grips.

Another unconventional approach to grips is counterweighting, a concept pioneered by Jack Nicklaus in the 1960s. Jack Wulkotte, who built and modified clubs for Nicklaus for decades, would pound a wooden plug into the end of his clubs and pour molten lead into the space until they achieved the desired weight. Nicklaus has said counterweighting helped take the hook out of his swing by slowing his hands down. In today's world, Sergio Garcia is one of only a handful of players using counterweights which is particularly helpful for players with a flatter swing plane as it makes the clubhead feel lighter at the top. Big picture, the argument for counterweighting is it creates a higher center of gravity, making the clubhead feel light which either 1) allows a player to swing faster or 2) allows a player to add additional weight to the clubhead and potentially swing slower, letting the mass of the clubhead create the distance instead of the swing speed. A more common implementation of this concept comes in the form of counterbalanced shafts. The theory is the same, but the method is slightly different as it involves the shaft construction itself and the extent of counterbalancing is likely less aggressive than putting weight in the butt of the grip. In recent years players like Tiger Woods, Justin Rose, and Rory McIlroy have put counterbalanced shafts in play. Overall, counterbalancing was a method used for years by arguably the best player in history, Jack Nicklaus, and it's a little bit of a head-scratcher it hasn't been more widely talked about or implemented in the subsequent decades.

Lastly, it's worth exploring the fact that the flagstick is now an optional piece of equipment for golfers. The rule change in 2019 allows golfers to keep the flagstick in while putting without penalty. The primary purpose was to facilitate faster play at the amateur and recreational levels, but the focus for many has become whether leaving the flagstick in increases or decreases the probability of sinking a putt. Both the science and art of it have been debated. On the science side, a large majority of studies, including ones done by putting guru Dave Pelz, have concluded keeping the flagstick in the hole results in a higher percentage of made putts and less distance for the second in case of a miss. This in addition to easier visualization on longer putts which has been going on for some time with caddies tending the flag.

While most studies do confirm the theoretical advantages of leaving the pin in, the benefits in practice are likely even higher. In scientific studies, putts are generally compared head-to-head when using the same speed and line in both scenarios, but in practice a player can change the line and speed depending on the circumstance. Imagine, for example, a three-foot slider downhill. Taking the pin out likely requires a player to play more break and at a slower putt speed, decreasing the likelihood of getting those two variables exactly right. Leaving the pin in allows a player to take some of the break out, hit it harder, and use the flag as a backstop. The combination likely increases the percentage chance of making it and in case of an off-center strike on the pin, the second putt probably comes to rest relatively close to the hole. It allows modern players to take a 1960s Arnold Palmer approach to short putts by simply ramming it in the back, an option that increasing green speeds had largely taken away over the decades.

Using the flagstick could be compared to a backboard in basketball. In 2011 a paper was published in the *Journal of Quantitative Analysis in Sports* by researchers from North Carolina State that demonstrated using the backboard yielded as much as a 20% higher shooting percentage from some angles than simply trying to execute a perfect nothing-but-net swoosh. Shots were analyzed from all distances and angles to the backboard with a vast majority of shot locations yielding anywhere from a 0 - 20% improvement in scoring percentage by using the backboard. The logic is intuitive and similar to the argument for the flagstick, both act as energy-absorbing aids in delivering the ball through the hoop or into a hole. As would be expected, the backboard became less helpful when shooting near the baseline where the backboard begins to disappear.[9]

Science-minded golfer Bryson DeChambeau analyzed it as follows: "It depends on the COR, the coefficient of restitution of the flagstick. In US Opens, I'll take it out, and every other Tour event, when it's fiberglass, I'll leave it in and bounce that ball against the flagstick if I need to." The practical implementation for most players will be situational, depending on the distance, break, green speed, wind, and flagstick composition.

On the art side, the optics for individual players can

have an equally powerful impact. Justin Thomas said, "I can't really take myself seriously if I keep the pin in," explaining it's hard for him to imagine attempting a winning putt on 18 with the flagstick sticking out of the cup. Golf is a mental game, something that seems to be amplified while putting. If leaving the pin in messes with a player psychologically or simply doesn't feel right, then any advantage from the physics of it might wither away in the mis-execution of a stroke.

In the first few seasons of play with the new rule, a majority of players continued to putt without the stick. Time will give us better data on the subject in tournament conditions and if that understanding confirms the earliest studies, there will likely be a gradual shift over time toward using the flagstick as a backstop. As with other equipment innovations discussed in this chapter, those willing to break with convention will have a competitive advantage for a period of time.

Out of the Box Bucket List:

☐ Play a round with single-length irons
☐ Use cavity-back clubs for 3-6 iron and blades for the 5-9 iron.
☐ Put two drivers in play
☐ Put four wedges in play
☐ Pull two long irons out of the bag
☐ Use a fat grip putter
☐ Use fat grips on irons and woods
☐ Try counterweight grips
☐ Try counterweight shafts
☐ Leave the flagstick in all round

CHAPTER 7
SEPARATION THROUGH STRENGTH

For years golf was considered by many to be merely a game, not a sport; and its participants simply players, not athletes. Historically the view was hard to challenge with broadcasts delivering images of overweight men waddling their way around a course, drink in one hand and cigar butt in the other. While the importance of hand-eye coordination was never doubted, overall fitness and strength were not seen as competitive advantages except to a select few.

Gary Player was a pioneer in this respect, a person who valued physical fitness from the beginning of his career and an example of its lifelong benefits. His pursuit of fitness started early in life when his brother Ian was leaving to fight in WWII. Gary shared his intention of becoming a professional athlete and Ian, seeing that he was going to be smaller than others, gave his weights to Gary and encouraged him to take care of his body and exercise for the rest of his life.

A man of faith, Gary said he adopted the attitude of treating his body like a temple. He refused large endorsement money from tobacco companies and drank little to no alcohol. He emphasized eating lots of fruits and vegetables and limited amounts of meats, carbs, and sugar. For most of his life, Gary drank a green smoothie daily consisting of spinach, kale, cucumber, celery, apple, lemon, and ginger. His strength training would include regular sessions of weight lifting, squats, sit-ups, and dumbbell exercises. On the road, Gary would be seen lifting weights at night, even the day before tournament rounds. Lifting weights back in that era was unconventional to say the least and he, as any pioneer does, faced criticism and ridicule. Gary would later reflect, "In the early part of my career, people thought I was an absolute nut for training with weights, but I stuck to my workout routine even during tournaments, and it paid off big time. Training the way I did gave me an edge no one could top because I knew I was in the best shape of anyone on tour."[1]

He earned the nickname "Mr. Fitness" in the 1950s and later wrote several books on the importance of exercise and golf performance. At his peak, Player was a modest 5'6'' and 155lbs, but his accomplishments towered over his colleagues landing him among the greatest to have ever played, winning three Masters, three Open Championships, two PGA Championships, and one US Open. As proof of his longevity, Gary points out he not only won the career Grand Slam on the regular tour but also on the senior tour.

While Jack Nicklaus was never the health equal of Gary

Player, he did have an awakening in 1969 at the Ryder Cup when he got tired for the first time in his life playing golf. It was no secret to him that he was overweight; the media wasn't shy about critiquing his physique calling him "fat Jack" and saying he looked "not so much like an athlete as a pile of clothes." It was compounded by the fact that during the 1960s Nicklaus was in the process of dethroning the widely loved Arnold Palmer and fans were not happy with him as the replacement. By self-admission Jack's appearance was raggedy; he wore old clothes, baggy shirts, and a crumpled hat. One journalist later recalled, "He was a fat kid who practically waddled when he walked. He looked like a sack of pork chops going down a fairway. His clothing fit him like a tent. He burped a lot. He had this crewcut that made him look like a two-ton shaving brush. People thought he had come to paint the clubhouse or move the dining room piano when he showed up for a tournament."[2] This all ended in 1969 when flying home from the Ryder Cup he announced he was going to lose 20 pounds and within a month he had dropped from 210 to a range where he would remain for the core of his career of 185-190 pounds. Regarding nutrition, Nicklaus had always taken a far from consensus approach when it came to drinking alcohol during tournaments. He later said, "I always felt drinking did not do well with nerves. The guys today don't do that. I never did that. Did I have a drink? Sure, here and there, but never while I was playing in tournaments. I always thought that was terrible for your nerves, and terrible for your touch, because I think the most important thing is to be totally there. I don't think guys did it because they were nervous, it was just their way of life. It was a social way of life, and golf was a social sport. Guys take the game today as more athletes, and I took it that way." [3]

As Arnold Palmer faded into history and Jack continued to win, Nicklaus's popularity increased dramatically over the decades and he became revered and admired among fans. How Jack's career would have played out differently had he remained overweight is hard to know; surely he still would have had success, but likely not to the same extent. It's noteworthy that the bulk of his major championships and PGA tour win count came after his 1969 weight loss.

Over the years, researchers have better quantified the benefits that proper nutrition can have on an athlete's physical performance. Alcohol has easily observed effects in drunk driving situations of slowing down vision and reaction time by as much as 25-30%. Even consumed in lower quantities, as was common among golfers in decades past, some degree of muscle coordination loss likely occurred resulting in higher scores. Jack probably did gain a legitimate edge over the field by avoiding alcohol during tournaments in the 1960s and '70s. Less perceptible, however, are the performance impacts of other types of dietary choices. In one study, marathon runners were divided into equally skilled groups based on a timed trial a couple of months before the race. One group was allowed to implement a freely chosen nutrition strategy while the other applied a scientifically based nutrition approach. The second group ran the marathon 4.7% faster than the first.[4] A similar study done with cyclists showed a 6%

improvement in time trial performance.[5] Yet another study showed a group of runners improved their 5k time by 6% after eating a Mediterranean-style diet in the days leading up to the race when compared to eating a Western-style diet. There are literally thousands of additional sports-related studies showing the performance benefits of a proper diet.

From the opposite perspective, the science is clear about the adverse effects of a poor diet. The prevalence of diabetes, heart attacks, hypertension, and back pain can go up 50-200% for people who are simply categorized as "overweight" (think 10-20lbs overweight) and as much as four times with regards to some health issues for people categorized as "obese."[6] A correlation has been found between high levels of blood sugar and muscle loss; in other words, consuming sugar or adhering to the associated lifestyle has the opposite effect of lifting weights in the gym.[7] People with more muscle than fat have been shown to better regulate their blood pressure, cope with stressful situations, and more quickly calm down from a tense episode than those with more fat. The ability to manage a stressful situation better than others would seem to be a useful advantage when playing the back nine of a major championship or even the local club championship for that matter.[8] There's also a demonstrated link between health and mental performance. One study of over 70,000 high school students showed overweight and obese teens have a statistically significant higher probability of having poor or very poor grades when compared to normal-weight peers.[9] Additionally, weight has been correlated with faster cognitive declines and increased risk for Alzheimer's disease.[10]   While some of these examples highlight the extremes, all of these factors could be looked at as a spectrum. Any improvement along the spectrum of health, nutrition, and exercise can translate into very meaningful improvements in athletic performance.

Greg Norman was the next notable health and nutrition advocate; even today he seems to be getting in better shape as the years progress. While on tour, he worked with a personal trainer which was not common during the '80s and '90s.   He was among the first after Gary Player to incorporate strength training as a regular part of his golf preparation. He had to buck convention because the self-appointed experts of his youth told Greg that exercising was bad for the golf swing. A lifetime later has proven the opposite to be true. In a 2003 book, Norman said, "Is golf ready for fitness? Yes! What was once the exception is becoming the rule, especially as we see the success of motivated, talented players who practice fitness training… Scan the pro tour statistics and you will see the difference between a person ranking 1st in the category and 25th or 30th could be as small as a quarter of a shot difference in scoring average. Multiplying that by four per round, however, shows that a small edge allows a player to win by one shot instead of losing by one shot. The other advantage to being fit is that when the body feels and functions well, the mind is more able to focus on the task at hand." Among the many benefits Norman accrued from maintaining a healthy body was being one of the longest, straightest drivers of his generation and being ranked number one in the world for a cumulative six years.

By the early 2000s, golfers were ready and soon compelled to become true athletes, a trend primarily driven by the arrival of a young player named Tiger Woods who would be a paradigm shifter in more ways than just fitness. Tiger turned professional in 1996 standing 6'2" tall, but weighing a skinny 158lbs with a 29" waist; only a few years later he had packed on 25 pounds of muscle through a strict workout routine and still boasted a very trim 31" waist.[11,12] For many years Tiger guarded his exercise habits like a state secret but, eventually, details emerged giving insights into his work ethic and personality. At his peak, he reportedly worked out six days a week for three-plus hours in a routine that included an overemphasis on stretching and flexibility, high-rep weight lifting, core/posture exercises, and cardio. Unlike other players, but much like Gary Player, Tiger enjoyed and thrived on his time in the gym. His coach, Hank Haney, recalled a time when Tiger showed up to the driving range and ran 50 yard sprints before their range practice session. Never enough, Woods is also widely known for training with Navy SEALs, learning how to clear buildings, rescue hostages, and navigate combat shooting courses.[13] While fitness had gained some inroads among PGA tour players since Gary Player, it was still relatively rare with Tiger recalling about his early days on tour, "There was no one in the gym, there was just me."

Nutrition was equally important to Tiger; he once explained on his website, "When it comes to eating right, I'm pretty easy to please. I stick to lean meats and seafood, lots of fruits and vegetables, and no junk food. My typical breakfast is an egg-white omelet with vegetables. Lunch and dinner are usually grilled chicken or fish with salad and vegetables. Protein ranks high in my diet because it helps build muscle tissue. I also take daily supplements for bone protection and nutritional support."

Tiger Woods 2019
Andrew Redington-Getty Images

Around the same time, Annika Sorenstam led the fitness revolution in women's golf. Having already experienced significant success through the '90s winning 18 LPGA tournaments, by the later part of the decade and early 2000s Sorenstam became increasingly interested in physical fitness. She hired a personal trainer who tailored a workout regime to include hundreds of core exercises per day, strength training, kickboxing, swimming, cycling, and running. Within a few years Annika increased her driving distance by 25 yards and went on to accumulate a total of 54 more LPGA tournament wins. Nancy Lopez, who turned pro in the late '70s, reflected, "When I was a rookie on tour, we didn't have the facilities we do today and I don't think any of us thought about fitness." That started to change, however, by the late 1990s with Lopez highlighting, "Annika Sorenstam set a precedent for what you need to do to stay in shape."[14] Annika herself speaking of fitness said, "In today's game, it's huge. It's always been important. I just don't think anybody thought it was that important. There are a few exceptions. Greg Norman and Gary Player many years ago were into it and that's why they've been so good and sustained it so long, but fitness is definitely a big part of the game. At the end of the day, it's so competitive that it's not enough to hit big drives and make putts. You have to stay in shape not only to prevent injuries but to stay strong with the heavy travel schedule."[15]

Annika Sorenstam 2008
Andrew Redington/ Getty Images

Unlike decades past, modern golfers have become true elite athletes. The examples are many and include the likes of Michelle Wie, Brooke Henderson, Sadena Parks, Lexi Thompson, Rory McIlroy, Justin Rose, Dustin Johnson,

Brooks Koepka, and Bryson DeChambeau among many more. Being fit is now less of a competitive advantage and more of a necessity to sustainably compete at the top of the golfing world.

Among elite athletes in golf today, Dustin Johnson ranks high on the list standing 6'4'' tall, 190lbs, with an average driving distance of 312 yards. He works out six days a week including a two hour gym session on tournament mornings. His trainer, Joey Diovisalvi, has him do a variety of strength training exercises that incorporate a lot of core. For example, instead of doing simple dumbbell presses, he'll execute them on an exercise ball alternating arms which requires a lot of core stabilization in the process. Instead of doing simple curls, he does them standing on one leg to simultaneously practice balance and strengthen the abdominal muscles. Dustin regularly throws a medicine ball against the wall, mimicking the motion of his backswing and follow through to help build golf-related muscles. He's commented, "With golf, it's all about consistency—you want to feel the same out there. The more I train, the stronger I feel, and the more mentally tough I become. For me, working out has as much to do with the mental aspect as it does the physical benefits. Working hard in the gym gives me confidence that when I'm on the course, even if it's been a long day out there, I can know that I'm going to feel the same when I finish as I did when I started."[17] For nutrition, Johnson hired a professional chef who prepares meals such as fish, vegetables, and quinoa while on the road.

A close friend of Dustin's and fitness training partner is

Brooks Koepka. The two have a brotherly relationship that includes a lot of trash talking and a constant stream of competitions to one-up each other. Brooks started working with golf fitness trainer Joey D in 2017 and subsequently won four major championships over the next two and a half years. His workouts are very similar to Dustin's which include the before-mentioned, as well as Olympic-style deadlifts, squats, and bench presses. Adding up the time spent in cardio, strength, stretching, and recovery, Brooks says he works on his body for four to five hours per day. This doesn't count any of the time spent on traditional range sessions, course practice, chipping, and putting greens. Koepka says the advantages of physical fitness in golf are mainly endurance focused; after four weeks of tournaments coming down the final nine on Sunday, he gains a lot of confidence from knowing he's fitter than most on tour.[18]

In another example, Rory McIlroy went through a well-known fitness transformation in 2011/12, having rarely been in the gym previously. He had been spending a lot of time around the professional tennis scene and realized just how much harder tennis players workout than golfers which gave him added motivation to hit the gym. At the time of his change, McIlroy said being in shape gave his golf swing more stability, the feel of fewer moving parts, and the freedom to swing harder without the fear of losing balance. One of the biggest benefits of being in shape came in the form of better posture which Rory says was terrible before implementing a workout regime. In the short span of 12 months, Rory went from having a soft, skinny, teenage-looking body to obtaining world-class athlete status. Starting with his 2011 US Open win, Rory went on a massive winning streak in the years to come that included four major championships which he has credited in part to his focus on fitness.

Those with an even greater ambition for physical superiority in golf can find a home in the World Long Drive Championships. It's hard to imagine that anyone can argue the top players of the world long drive circuit aren't athletes. They look more like football or hockey players than golfers with muscles bursting out of their shirts, bodies built like oxen, and drives that consistently top 400 yards. Two-time world champion Tim Burke is 6'5", 235lbs of muscle with a longest drive of 474 yards. Sandra Carlborg, who was previously a personal trainer, is a five-time world long drive champion with a longest drive of 401 yards. These long drive competitors produce so much clubhead speed that often their feet aren't even touching the ground at impact as a normal stance can't handle the forward momentum. Arnold Palmer, who was known for his lunging all-out attack on the ball, said, "There's nothing in golf more spectacular and satisfying to the soul and the senses than a perfectly long and straight drive ... a long drive is good for the ego (...) I've said previously, what other people may find in poetry or in art museums I find in the flight of a good drive."[19]

The majority of the world's top golfers today have bought into the concept and importance of physical fitness to varying degrees, but plenty of room is still open for innovators to gain an edge. Even in a sport as obviously physical as football (where teams have full-time doctors, physical therapists, and trainers) some players are still finding competitive advantages by thinking and doing things differently. Tom Brady and his body coach, Alex Guerrero, have taken an entirely new approach to workouts and recovery that hasn't come without a significant amount of ridicule and controversy. As Brady explains in his recent book, the conventional approach to strength training in football might itself be the root cause of injury and shortened careers.

Traditionally, football players lift increasingly heavy free weights and recover by icing muscles after practice. This cycle creates short, dense, tight muscles that put a strain on tendons, joints, and ligaments; increase inflammation; and make a player's body less able to absorb hits and shocks. Brady, on the other hand, has an intense focus on pliability before and after his workout. Pliability is a process of lengthening and softening muscles through deep-force muscle work or rollers. The concept being in order to keep the body in balance, the process of muscle tightening through strength training needs to be properly balanced with muscle softening and lengthening. This puts less strain on joints, enables the body to absorb hits without injury, and gives muscles more room to make effective contracting motions during play.

Conventionally, football players lift free weight in motions that may or may not resemble those used during play. Brady, on the other hand, will spend 90% of his strength training time with resistance bands in motions that resemble those used on the field. Bands allow for more varied exercise paths than weight machines which have a very fixed track. Training with bands is a practical approach to strength that zeroes in on precise objectives rather than aimless efforts to generally get stronger. Typically, football players will lift the maximum weight possible, in few reps, at slow speeds. Brady, on the other hand, lifts less weight, at higher rep counts, and at "the speed of play." Using less weight reduces the wear and tear on joints and going at faster speeds trains muscles to respond as will be needed in game-like situations. Brady also takes unconventional approaches to brain training, hydration, tech-enabled sleepwear, and nutrition. The conventional approach to football strength training results in an average NFL career duration of fewer than five years while Brady's approach is geared toward longevity and durability.[20]

Like most out-of-the-box thinkers, Tom and Alex were willing to learn from the accumulated knowledge of their sport but also were open to the possibility that everyone was getting it wrong in certain aspects. Love him or hate him, in most statistical categories Brady has improved with age, continues to take his team to the Super Bowl year after year, and has more rings than any other quarterback (or NFL team for that matter) in history. Lest anyone believe no more room for physical differentiation in golf exists, we only have to look at football to see the open space for players willing to do something differently.

Pulling it all together, it's clear that today's golfers can truly be classified as athletes in every sense of the word. Golf has evolved from what some considered simply a pastime or game into a legitimate athletic sport, and recently an Olympic sport. While less so than in the past, there is still plenty of room to gain a physical edge in golf for those willing to think out of the box.

Out of the Box Bucket List:

- ☐ Believe health impacts your golf score
- ☐ Make weight lifting and cardio an important golf preparation routine
- ☐ Combine core stability with other exercises in your workout
- ☐ Cross train with other sports to improve golf
- ☐ Eat healthy foods
- ☐ Avoid alcohol
- ☐ Try Tom Brady style workout: pliability & resistance band emphasis
- ☐ Employ low weight, high rep workout regimes

CHAPTER 8
MENTAL GAME MAVERICKS

Golf is undoubtedly a mental game. Bobby Jones once famously commented, "Golf is played mainly on a five-and-a-half-inch course, the space between your ears." There's probably no better indication of the mental nature of golf than the superstitions that exist among even elite golfers. Ernie Els is well known for only playing a number two ball and throwing it out after a birdie because he believes every ball only has one birdie in it. Kerrie Webb has a lucky ball marker she's used for 15 years and her caddie knows losing it would result in getting fired. Jack Nicklaus played golf only if he had exactly three coins in his pocket, no more, no less. Several players have superstitions around the placement of their ball marker, a few making sure the head of the coin is pointed toward the hole. Lastly, tee color seems to be a theme with some professionals only using one color of tee and others avoiding a specific color.

It could be argued that golf is more mental than most sports given the relatively slow nature and overall duration of play. A basketball player has a repository of learned and practiced skills such as the cross-over, base-line drive, three-pointer, pump-fakes, among many others. During a basketball game, much of what occurs is reactionary to the opportunities presented. The game is played so quickly that the mind has very little time to contemplate what to do, a great basketball player will intuitively react to given situations. For example, a point guard might see his defender drop one foot back while the other side of the court clears; a split second period of time might open to capitalize on the opportunity with a small fake, cross over and drive to the basket. Basketball players don't have the luxury to ponder or mull over what's going on; it's largely a reactionary game. That doesn't mean mental toughness is absent from basketball, it just means the nature of the challenge is constructed differently.

On the other hand, contemplate the nature of golf where each player might have three to four minutes of thinking time between each shot. At address, a golfer might take 10-15 seconds to set up, look at the target, and prepare before pulling back. The golf swing itself lasts almost a full second, enough time to second guess, change paths, pull it, push it, or double cross. Additionally, very few sports competitions last four to five hours; it's the equivalent of a mental marathon. There is no better example of how psychological golf can become than the yips, a condition that leaves players unable to make the simplest of shots - a two to three foot putt. It's hard to comprehend the yips are even possible for a life-long trained athlete.

The mind, however, is unfortunately influenced by external factors in greater ways and more often than most want to admit. Consider for a moment the home-team bias in sports. Whether it's the NFL, NBA, MLB, or NHL, in most years home teams have won between 55-60% of the time. In theory, this number should be 50%, but there's something psychologically beneficial about playing in a familiar place in front of a friendly, positive crowd.

A study done on rugby players sheds some light on this topic. The players were divided into two groups a couple of hours before a game; the first was shown video clips of great plays they had made in the previous game with the coaches providing positive commentary. The players in the second group were shown video clips of poor plays from the previous game and given negative feedback. The first group's testosterone levels increased and those players had better game stats than the second group, who had decreased levels of testosterone and performed worse in the game. The study was replicated under varying circumstances with similar results. The experiment shows just how influential even small amounts of positive and negative feedback can be for athletes.[1]

With that context, it makes sense that on a larger scale, the positive feedback of thousands of cheering, adoring fans could impact the performance of even elite athletes across multiple sports. This thesis was confirmed in the '20/'21 COVID-protocol-filled NFL season when, for the first time in history, home teams had a sub 50% win percentage. The empty stadiums had a quantifiable negative impact on home teams, those cardboard cutouts just weren't the same as cheering fans!

Golfers face a different set of circumstances than most athletes. While large galleries attend tournaments, they are generally neutral to positive in their feedback. In other sports, teams face off directly against each other at the same time, while in golf they go out in groups of as little as two at varying times throughout the day. In many ways, golf is structured to be a game played more against oneself than it is directly against other players. Varying strategies are employed to seize control of the environment and reduce the influence of external factors. In 2008 Trevor Immelman led the Masters going into the final round in which he decided not to look at a scoreboard the entire day. He focused on staying in the moment and the next task at hand. Standing on the 18th green he leaned over to his caddie and asked where they stood to which he responded, "three strokes ahead of Tiger." Immelman's solution for controlling one external factor was simply to eliminate it from the round.

If we look back through history and gauge the importance of mental game training by the number of books published on the subject, there was little emphasis in the '60s, '70s, and '80s. There were obviously players who appreciated its value such as Gary Player, Arnold Palmer, and Jack Nicklaus, but wider adoption of formalized mental game training methods didn't occur until later. Only a handful of golf books on the mental game had been published before the mid-1990s when an explosion of interest occurred driven primarily by Dr. Bob Rotella. He was the most prolific writer on the subject and gained a large following of tour players during the time. Rotella was one of the most influential pioneers in mental game training and some of his earliest students included Tom Kite, Pat Bradley, Nick Price, and Brad Faxon. Since the 1990s the number of books and academic studies on golf psychology has exploded, paving the way for players to experiment and differentiate themselves in their mental game approach.

Today players are using everything from cutting-edge brain training techniques to working on innovative ways to perfect long understood mental game philosophies. The strategies can broadly be bucketed into visualization, triggers, routines, brain training, breathing, and intimidation.

Visualization/ Imagery

At the 2008 Summer Olympics Michael Phelps was in pursuit of history, an eventual eight gold medals, when he dove into the water for the 200 butterfly and his goggles broke, slowly filling with water until he was essentially blind. When his hand touched the final wall he pulled the broken goggles off to find out he had not only won gold, but had set a new world record. Phelps would later credit his performance in part to mental preparation. For most of his career, Michael spent two hours a day ahead of a big swim race mentally constructing it in his head, visualizing in precise detail the dive, glide, stroke, reaching the wall, flipping, and the final push. When the unexpected happened in 2008, he was still able to execute. Elite athletes in many sports have used visualization techniques to improve performance. While difficult to verify for sure, the way these champions talk about their imagery routines and the length of time dedicated to that preparation makes it very likely they are going above and beyond the competition.

Rock climber Alex Honnald, famous for his free solo ascent of Yosemite's El Capitan, has often explained visualization is essential to overcoming the fear inherent in climbing without a rope. Without mental preparation, a free solo climber is susceptible to panic, fear, and ultimately the very real possibility of a fatal mistake while hanging thousands of feet off the ground. Weeks ahead of a free solo, a climber will physically practice the route with a rope, but practically speaking, only so many runs can be done. Visualization allows a climber to mentally increase the number of practice climbs by many multiples and account for a wide variety of possible scenarios. Neuroscientists have shown that imagining something in great detail in the mind fires up the same neural pathways that would activate in real life. In an intense, detailed imaging session, the body will react with the same stress response and adrenaline release as would occur in real life which allows athletes to practice coping responses and perfecting athletic techniques.

Alex Honnald said, "Sitting and thinking hour after hour. Visualizing every single move, everything that could possibly happen. That's what it takes to wrap your mind around a challenge such as the one I was about to attempt. That's what I mean by preparation... In a real sense, I performed the hard work of that free solo during the days leading up to it. Once on the climb, it was just a matter of executing."[2]

In addition to these high-profile examples, literally hundreds of scientific research papers back up the benefits of imagery training and sports performance. The results of these types of studies for golfers have been no different. One experiment on bunker shot accuracy divided a group of avid, sub-five handicap competitive golfers into four groups. The control group, the physical practice group, the imagery practice group, and the physical + imagery group. The object was to improve bunker shots accuracy as measured by 15 shots. The control group was given a book to read; the physical practice group was told to practice bunker shots twice a week for a prescribed amount of time; the imagery group was told to simply imagine practicing bunker shots twice a week for the same amount of time; and the last group was told to both physically and mentally practice bunker shots twice a week. As might be expected, the group that did both visual and physical practice saw the most improvement, while the control showed no improvement. Most interestingly, however, the group told to mentally practice bunker shots achieved nearly the same amount of improvement in accuracy as the group that actually physically practiced bunker shots. Visualization in this case was essentially as beneficial as actual physical practice![3]

Kathy Whitworth said in her book, "Visualization was a big thing for me. Another way I used visualization was in my mind's eye I could see myself on the driving range hitting balls. I'd see myself swinging with what I was working on, or what I needed to be working on. Then I'd go out to the range and try to do what I visualized in the room. At times I could hit it pretty darn good in my mind!"[4] Kathy was obviously one of the greatest golfers of all time with 88 LPGA tour wins including six major championships.

Jack Nicklaus in the mid-1970s wrote, "I never hit a shot, even in practice, without having a very sharp, in-focus picture of it in my head. It's like a color movie. First I 'see' the ball where I want it to finish, nice and white and sitting up high on the bright green grass. Then the scene quickly changes and I 'see' the ball going there; it's path, trajectory, and shape, even its behavior on landing. Then there is sort of a fade out, and the next scene shows me making the kind of swing that will turn the images into reality"[5] While it can't be known for sure, it's highly unlikely other professional golfers in the 1970s were visualizing to the same depth and precision as Jack. His unconventional use of mental imagery, whether purposeful or naturally occurring, was likely a competitive advantage.

In 2015 the golfing world took greater notice of a pre-shot routine Jason Day had been working to perfect over the years. Partially inspired by Aaron Baddeley, Jason stood behind the ball, closed his eyes for a few seconds to visualize the shot, and then approached the ball to swing. While he had done something similar since his teenage years, there seemed to be more thought, intention, and dedication to the process that year. He later explained, "When I close my eyes and I see a picture of myself. I visualize my swing go back, then go through, and then I see the ball come out. I see how it goes, where it lands, and how it bounces... I make sure I don't hit the shot, or don't stop visualizing until I'm fully comfortable with that visual."[6] It was in this 2015-2016 period that Jason won eight times including the PGA Championship and Players Championship and was ranked number one in the world.

Visualization was important to many other elite golfers throughout history. Gary Player said, "I do quite a lot of meditating. I associate meditating with visualization to a great degree." Ray Floyd, who was known for his mental toughness, said, "I honestly believe with a strong mind you can literally 'will' the ball into the hole." During a time when Phil couldn't play golf for a couple of months he said, "Mental rehearsal is just as important as physical rehearsal." While it's hard to compare what happens in the heads of different professional golfers, quotes from these top-level players can give us fairly high confidence that their use of visualization was an unconventional competitive advantage.

Triggers

In 2010 Louis Oosthuizen was having a hard time concentrating in the moment, his mind wandered all over the place. He needed a trigger to get back in the moment and sports psychologist Karl Morris asked him to come up with a word that describes the feeling he wanted to have during a round. Louis responded with "concentration" to which Karl asked what color he would assign to that word.

Louis said "red" and then Karl suggested he put a red dot on his glove. It could have been anything, but the red dot was Louis's signal to focus, forget about distractions, and play the shot. Within a month he won the 2010 Open Championship at St. Andrews.

Elite golfers throughout history have used triggers as a means to eliminate outside distractions, focus, and shift the swing into gear. Gary Player was famous for kicking in his right knee which served as a catalyst for his swing to start. Nancy Lopez would raise her hands up four to five inches immediately before hitting such that her arm and shaft produced a straight line. The motion unique to her served as a mechanism to initiate the swing. Phil Mickelson uses a forward press just before putting. Sam Snead described the advantages of his forward press as follows: "For my money, the single most important device for getting nerves and muscles ready to execute the golf swing properly is the forward press. I've never made a golf swing that did not start from a forward press, and I've never met a golfer who failed to play better after learning to trigger his swing this way."[7]

Sports psychologists will say an effective trigger doesn't have to be a physical movement. Like Louis Oosthuizen, it could be a visual cue. It could also be a word or phrase. Positive self-talk, like visualization, is another well-studied and proven method to enhance sports performance. Greg Norman was one of the more notable self-talkers on tour, building himself up with audible positive messages before and after a shot all with the goal of keeping his mind in a positive frame.

Routine

Routines are valuable in golf and life because they automate repeatable tasks. A sense of familiarity and ease accompany the known, as is the case with the home field advantage discussed earlier. Routines in golf come in various forms such as warm-up routines, pre-shot routines, and intra-shot routines. They all create a sense of consistency and confidence which results in better outcomes.

Among the most unconventional warm-up routines in golf is that of Miguel Angel Jimenez. He was deemed "The Most Interesting Man in Golf" due to his resemblance to the personality and image of The Most Interesting Man in the World in the well-known beer ad campaign. Fans have jokingly commented, "I don't always stretch, but when I do, it's like Miguel Angel Jimenez." He's a Spaniard who sports long curly hair pulled back in a ponytail, loves to smoke cigars, drink wine, and drive fast cars. He sheathes his imaginary sword/putter after making important putts, somewhat reminiscent of Chi Chi Rodriquez. Jimenez is one of the biggest characters in the golfing world and fans love his unique, no-filter personality. His stretching routine includes twirling clubs in front of him to loosen the wrists, squatting down so that his butt is nearly touching the ground, and most famously he brings his knees together and circulates them in a motion that looks more like a dance move than a stretch. Fans can't handle it, breaking out into applause on the driving range as he proceeds through his stretching sequence. While Miguel's warm-up progression is highly unorthodox, golf fitness gurus applaud the routine saying it loosens the muscles more effectively than the way other players stretch before their round.

On the LPGA tour, Sadena Parks for a time had her own unique warm-up routine. It consisted of alternating leg lunges while doing various hand movements including one that resembled raising the roof dance move. Her routine blurred the lines of stretching and dancing making it a fan favorite scene. While unconventional, it was arguably a very effective stretching routine that warmed up the body better than what other LPGA tour players implemented. Sadena is a true athlete having excelled in a variety of sports growing up including basketball where she once aspired to be a WNBA player and was featured on *ESPN the Magazine's Body Issue* in 2015. Perhaps in the future more players will warm up like Sadena and Miguel.

Another routine in golf is that which occurs right before a shot. In basketball, several studies have confirmed that the use of a well-defined pre-shot routine leads to a higher free throw shooting percentage whether implemented in a controlled environment or real game situation. When researchers asked participants to alter or change the length of their pre-shot routine, their shooting percentage went down.[8] For golfers, a pre-shot routine serves the same purpose as many mental game strategies which is to limit distractions, doubts, and promote consistency.

Among the most unique in golf is the putt-reading pose of Camilo Villegas. In his home country of Colombia, they call him "el hombre arana" or spider man for the way he balances his body hovering horizontally about three inches off the ground, face nearly touching the green surface as he analyzes the break of a putt from a vantage point most golfers will never experience. It all started in 2006 when Camilo was struggling with his putter. He figured if he could get a better read on the putt it could improve his performance so right in the middle of the round he dropped down, liked the feel, and has done it ever since. It's a feat of strength and flexibility in addition to requiring a healthy amount of self-confidence. Camilo says, "Everyone makes fun of me for the way I read putts, I'm just trying to get the ball in the hole." Even if his odd putt-reading style results in one extra putt made over the course of a four-day tournament, it would be worth the effort and barbs that come his way.

Lastly, the way players spend their time between shots happens to constitute most of a golf round. Every player has a different routine; some chat up the crowd and make jokes, like Lee Trevino, while others walk in quiet solitude. Bob Rotella once commented, "The toughest player, mentally and emotionally, I've ever worked with is Pat Bradley, the LPGA Tour Hall of Famer. She was like Ben Hogan – she didn't talk to anybody when she played. She told me she didn't have time to chat with players because she had an ongoing dialogue with herself." After her first six seasons on the LPGA tour, Pat Bradley was frustrated she couldn't finish on Sunday, often coming in just behind the leader. She came up with a strategy of positive self-talk during the round to calm her nerves and keep focused. By 1986 she was in the hunt at the Dinah Shore with the real prospect of winning a major championship. Bradley said to keep herself under control she had tunnel vision and repeatedly gave herself intra-round pep talks, a strategy that ultimately worked as she captured the title.[9]

Next Generation Brain Training

Every person has a different capacity to cope with stressful situations. At the extreme end, free solo climber Alex Honnold had MRI brain scans done which concluded by and large he does not feel fear or at least nowhere near the same level as other humans. For Alex, this is probably a major reason he can hang off a 2,000-foot cliff with handholds the width of a pencil and not completely flip out like everyone else would in the same situation. While genetics explain some of one's capacity to cope with stress, scientists are learning it's also a skill that can be acquired and learned.

Bryson DeChambeau is unsurprisingly pushing the boundaries on mental training techniques. He travels with a small mental training system which, as he described in a press conference, helps him manage the parasympathetic and sympathetic states of his mind. The sympathetic nervous system is activated when a person encounters a stressful, exciting, dangerous, intense, or other similar circumstance. It's often referred to as the "fight or flight" response and could be activated in situations ranging from nearly getting hit by a car to getting yelled at to standing over a critical shot during a golf match. The sympathetic system is preservational, increasing the heart rate and releasing hormones designed to implement a "fight or flight" solution to the perceived problem. While that might actually be helpful in some combative sports such as football or boxing, it is detrimental for golfers where the ability to run faster or physically attack someone is not a viable solution. Golfers need to be able to control their body's natural response to stress and activate the parasympathetic system which is responsible for calming the body down.

Like any other desired skill, athletes can practice controlling their natural emotional responses. For Bryson, the brain training system he uses consists, in part, of watching a movie and seeking to keep his body in a parasympathetic (calm) state. Particularly in an action movie, there will be fight scenes, surprises, intense situations and, while everyone knows they are not real, the mind gets caught up in the storyline and the body reacts accordingly. This sets up a virtual simulation in which Bryson can practice having his body transition between sympathetic and parasympathetic states and gaining more control over that process. His success is measured by an EEG sensor sitting on his head which detects the level of electrical activity in the brain. The theory is the skills practiced in a virtual setting can be translated into real-life situations on the golf course.

Breathing

Deep breathing is one of the most practical techniques for activating the parasympathetic system and calming the body down. The practice has ancient roots, documented as far back as 500-700BC to Indian yoga texts which referred to it as *pranayama*. Separated into its components, pran means "life force" and ayama means "expansion or extension"; together the breathing technique was understood to be the "expansion of the life force." It became the fourth of the eight limbs of yoga and has been practiced for thousands of years since by various cultures.[10]

The benefits of deep breathing have been demonstrated in both the short and long term which includes lower heart rates, lower cortisol levels, and a general feeling of being more relaxed and less stressed.[11] Additionally, breathing exercises have been shown to reduce blood pressure and fatigue, and to increase a person's ability to maintain attention and focus. Breathing techniques have been deployed to aid people in a variety of ways including combating depression, ADHD, anxiety, stress, and health issues.[12] The advice to "take a deep breath" might be dismissed as a trivial solution for those not acquainted with the science backing it up. Those who have seen the immense amount of scientific validation for this coping strategy understand its potential to improve mental performance.

In 2017 Jason Dufner won the Memorial helped by a sniper-inspired breathing strategy while putting. Before the tournament, Jason's friend sent him an article that talked about how important breathing patterns are for military snipers trying to reduce their heart rate, calm tension, and ultimately make a more accurate shot. For Dufner, in addition to those calming benefits, it gave him something to focus on that shielded distractions from entering his mind.

Lexi Thompson has made breathing exercises part of her weekly mental preparation routine. She does breathing sequences before arriving on property, again just before the first tee, and then throughout the round to maintain calmness. After paying more attention to her breathing Lexi had realized that without a purposeful focus on it, her breathing would get shallow and short, a very natural response to stress and intensity.[13]

Jason Day is another great example of implementing a breathing strategy that fits seamlessly into his pre-shot routine. While standing behind the ball he takes a deep, diaphragmatic breath; visualizes the shot with his eyes closed; then steps up to address the ball. The deep breath catalyzes a biological response lowering Day's blood pressure, heart rate, and cortisol levels. In that state, he has prepared his mind for vivid shot visualization more deliberate in its purpose than most professionals. As Jason Day approaches the ball he's executed one of the best pre-shot mental preparations of any golfer on tour, giving him the highest likelihood to perform at peak capacity.

Intimidation

Golf is among the politest of sports, particularly compared to the fistfights of hockey, the bench-clearing brawls of baseball, and the line of scrimmage trash talking in football. That doesn't mean, however, golfers throughout history haven't taken advantage of intimidation tactics.

Wearing a red shirt on Sunday has been Tiger's personal tradition from the beginning of his professional career. He explains, "I wear red on Sundays because my mom thinks that that's my power color, and you know you should always listen to your mom." Psychologically, colors have been proven to evoke certain emotions with red being associated with extremes including anger, power, dominance, love, passion, intensity, danger, and warning. Wearing red likely boosts Tiger's own self-confidence while simultaneously sending off turbulent emotions to those around him. Red is also easily seen from a distance, forcing players across the course to cope with the subtle mental attack.

An absolutely fascinating study done by Durham University showed sports competitors wearing red uniforms have a higher win percentage than those wearing other colors. In the 2004 Olympic Games competitors in various combat sports were randomly assigned red or blue uniforms and the red group won 55% of the head-to-head matches. Separately, a controlled experiment of combat athletes showed those wearing red had higher heart rates and overall strength during competition. Further, a study of the English Football League spanning 1946 to 2003 showed 60% of league champions were from teams wearing predominantly red uniforms. Lastly, human judges picked players pictured wearing red uniforms over those wearing blue uniforms as most likely to win 60% of the time. In summary, red is scientifically proven to improve the performance of the person wearing it, intimidate competitors facing it, and create a bias among referees and judges for it.[14] Players unfortunate enough to have been paired with Tiger over the years played .46 strokes worse compared to their personal average, a quantification of the Tiger intimidation factor.[15] For professionals and amateurs alike it seems wearing red on tournament day is the logical choice.

Other golfers throughout history have used subtle intimidation to their benefit. Raymond Floyd was notably intense, with Nick Price once recalling, "He was intimidating on the golf course, not because of his personality, but more because of his intensity as a professional. He was as intense on the course as anyone I ever played with. Raymond was always business on the course, always." Mark O'Meara recalled Floyd was "the most intimidating player I've ever played against. He plays every shot like it's the last shot of his life. He's like a black leopard, stalking the jungle."[16]

Then there was the 1971 US Open playoff between Jack Nicklaus and Lee Trevino. During the week Trevino had stashed a rubber snake in his bag to entertain the gallery and poke fun at Merion's extremely high rough. Always a joker, Trevino pulled out the snake on the first tee of their 18 hole playoff and, at Jack's request, threw it on the ground next to him. The gallery was roaring in laughter and Jack smiled at the situation, but with his arms extended stiffly and face strained, the tenseness of Jack's body language was hard to miss. Both have since brushed off the scene as good-natured fun, but at the end of the day, it might have thrown Jack off his game for a few holes. He uncharacteristically bogeyed the second and double bogeyed the third, going on to eventually lose to Trevino by three strokes.

Today golfers walk a fine line of subtle intimidation mostly done in a passive aggressive way with a safety net of plausible deniability. It comes in the form of standing just close enough to a competitor on the tee box to irritate them, but far enough away that it could be viewed as nothing at all. It manifests in the form of walking ahead on a hole so they are in the peripheral vision of their competitor's next shot. It comes in standing just enough behind a player on the green so that their presence is noted but not construed as unsportsmanlike. Overall, golf is still very high on the sportsmanship spectrum, hopefully a defining characteristic that will persist through time, but every once in a while the competitive juices get flowing and some gamesmanship comes out.

Overall, golf is a very mental game and the modern player can't ignore the potential to increase performance by mastering the mind. Moe Norman probably summed it up best when he said, "Good thinking, good golf, bad thinking, bad golf. Bad thinking hurts more than bad swinging."[17] Luckily for professional and amateur golfers alike, the mental game can be practiced, worked on, and improved. Arnold Palmer once commented, "Success in golf depends less on the strength of your body than upon strength of mind."

Out of the Box Bucket List:

☐ Spend 30 minutes visualizing a round before playing

☐ Visualize each shot before hitting it

☐ Use personal triggers for increased concentration

☐ Talk to yourself during the round in a positive way

☐ Stretch like Miguel or Sedena

☐ Read putts like Camilo

☐ Take a deep breath before every shot

☐ Wear a red shirt, shorts, and hat to your next tournament

☐ Practice controlling the transition between parasympathetic and sympathetic states using brain training software

☐ Practice *pranayama* or breathing techniques as a normal pattern of life

CHAPTER 9
AN ANALYTICAL EDGE

Golf is both an art and a science. On one hand, golf demands creativity, feel, touch, and imagination. Golf is unique among major sports in that the playing field is ever-changing – every week professional players compete on a different course, at varying altitudes, in a range of temperatures and weather conditions. The same course can be set up using different tee boxes, pin locations, green speeds, and rough lengths. The variability leads to an incalculable number of possible shots and responses to those situations.

Sometimes the most creative shots come from players who have found themselves in a bit of trouble. Who can forget Sergio Garcia's closed-eye shot next to the tree in the PGA, or Phil's Mickelson's shot from the pine straw on Augusta's 13th, or Seve Ballestarous's knee shot under the tree? Players have hit shots from the grandstands, from high up off tree branches, bounced off walls, and stripped down out of the water. The need for creativity and art is part of what makes golf so enjoyable and captivating.

Golf will never lose its need for creativity, but as is happening in other sports, the science of the game is becoming an increasingly important piece of the equation. In baseball, the importance of advanced analytics for recruiting and team construction was detailed in Michael Lewis's book *Moneyball*, later made into a movie. The story of Billy Beane and the Oakland A's in the early 2000s showed that ingrained methods used by coaches and scouts to evaluate baseball players were biased in old traditions not supported by data. Constrained by one of the lowest budgets in MLB, Billy Beane took a revolutionary approach to recruiting players rooted in big data analysis and a value-for-results framework. The efforts took the A's to the playoffs in 2002/ 2003 and changed baseball forever.

In today's golf world players who ignore data, advanced analytics, and precision measurement trackers do so at their own peril. Tools like ShotLink, Trackman, and smartwatches/clubs/balls are to golf as the crossbow and catapult were to ancient warfare.

Use of the traditional bow and arrow can be found among the earliest records of human history, dating back to tribal times of hunting and gathering. It later became a reliable wartime weapon for thousands of years powered by the arm strength and coordination of its user. In many ways more effective than those engaging in hand-to-hand combat, skilled bowmen were hard to come by as they required years of training and a person of abnormal upper body strength. Sometime between 400 and 600 BC a revolutionary new weapon emerged among Chinese and Greek armies called the crossbow. The crossbow was more powerful, superior in accuracy, and easier to use than the old bow and arrow. Common peasants could be trained in a few weeks to be as effective in war as veteran bowmen. The speed produced by a crossbow could pierce armor at ranges unattainable by a traditional arrow and could be cocked and left ready to fire for long periods of time, whereas a bowman would fatigue in just a few minutes of keeping a bow drawn, ready for action. Lastly, it was remarkably accurate and easy to shoot given it could be rested upon a shield and steadied with two hands instead of one.

Even with the overwhelming evidence in favor of using the crossbow, there were skeptics. Some nobility opposed it because it empowered peasants and others simply held on to old ways, reluctant to accept new technology often to their own detriment. The crossbow was the predecessor to a class of weapons often referred to as catapults, machines used to hurl large projectiles towards opposing forces or castles. Catapults, in the beginning, were essentially very large crossbows, but eventually developed into huge medieval trebuchets able to hurl 200-300 hundred pound stones a 1000 feet or more. Each of these inventions revolutionized the battlefield and armies that quickly adopted benefitted from their advantages.

In its own sphere, golf is currently experiencing an unprecedented pace of innovation and invention, among the most important being Trackman and similar swing analytic devices. In 2003 two brothers, Klaus and Morten

Eldrup-Jorgensen, teamed up with Carsten Hallas and Fredrik Tuxen to form Trackman. Tuxen was a radar engineer who brought experience in missile-tracking systems and all were avid golfers or lovers of the game. They set out with the objective of creating a highly accurate doppler tracking system for analyzing ball flights and golf swings. After a few years of development, they started pitching their product to club manufacturers who immediately saw the value (even though it cost a couple hundred thousand at the time) because the system far surpassed anything that had been built before. Factors such as attack angle, swing path, clubhead speed, ball trajectory, spin, and shape could be measured with pinpoint accuracy. This created an objective standard on which hundreds of unbiased studies of the golf swing would be based in the years to come.

By 2007 Trackmans began appearing on PGA Tour driving ranges with adoption accelerating in a pronounced way roughly five to six years later. Historically, coaches used videotape recordings and did their best to visually diagnose a player's problem, but it was largely a subjective process based on feel; it was an art. Trackman brought science to golf. Armed with data, forward-thinking golf coaches started to debunk old myths and gain new insights about the golf swing.

One example is our understanding of what creates a draw or fade. Many people have been taught that to hit a draw one needs to close the clubface more than normal (relative to the target) and swing inside out and vice versa for a fade; some have summed it up as "the path sends it, the face bends it." Tools like Trackman have debunked this old view, showing that the clubface is responsible for 70-80% of the flight direction while the swing path relative to the clubface is what creates the spin. In other words, to hit a draw the clubface actually needs to be open at impact! The trick simply being the swing path needs to be even more open (inside-out) than the clubface. This is counter-intuitive and opposite of how most think about draws and fades, yet it's hard to argue with precision data. The truth would be more closely described as "the clubface sends it, the path bends it." The open clubface will produce a shot that starts right of the target but has the side spin necessary to draw it back to the hole. It's these types of breakthroughs in understanding that can help improve swings and scores.[1]

This principle holds true for putting as well. A square putter face to the target at impact has a disproportionately large effect on the direction of a putt than the swing path. This knowledge can meaningfully refocus practice sessions to what matters most.

After Billy Beane started using big data, his baseball scouts could no longer simply lean back in a chair and pontificate about the merits of this player or that. Asserting that a baseball player would be successful because he had a "good face" was no longer a justifiable reason for a draft pick. Similarly, during this time, it became increasingly hard for golf coaches to have credibility if they couldn't back up their opinions and golf swing theories with unbiased Trackman data.

Among the earliest adopters of Trackman on the LPGA

tour were Michelle Wie and Anna Nordqvist. On the PGA tour, it was coach Sean Foley and many of his tour pros at the time including Tiger Woods, Justin Rose, and Hunter Mahan. The system completely changed the way coaches interacted with players. Early on Foley explained, "It saves time all the way around because I can do now in two weeks what would have taken me two months of trial and error. The advantage is because the numbers are there and because the numbers are correct, the trust aspect of the relationship between the student and coach goes up too. That trust aspect is probably the most important part for learning."[2] Trackman was to golf what the crossbow was to warfare; in a nutshell, Trackman accelerated learning, improvement, and ultimately performance. In business terms, it was the definition of a competitive advantage for those willing to adopt it quickly. Even six years after introduction in 2013, reportedly less than 30% of tour players owned a Trackman. In hindsight, it seems foolish that one would choose to ignore a major technological advancement, but this has been a common story throughout much of human history with regard to innovation.[3]

Tiger Woods explained the advantages this way: "Understanding those numbers is relevant because it's pure numbers, there's no getting around it. They're universal, they're law."[5] He later elaborated, "A lot of times what we're feeling that we are doing is not exactly what we're doing. I just think you're trying to match up feel and real, and as you make swing changes, you make slight alterations, and you start realizing what the club is doing at impact and what that can translate into in the performance of a golf ball."[4]

Even with high-profile adopters, there were and are many skeptics. They primarily harp on the complexity of the approach, the technical focus, perceived rigidness of the endeavor, and the need for art and feel in the golf swing. While they make some valid points and a certain amount of balance is necessary, history is not on their side when looking at the adoption and success of advanced analytics across many sports and businesses in today's world. Analytics will likely be just as important to amateurs as they are for professionals in the years to come. While the price tag of a Trackman system is out of reach for most, cheaper alternatives are emerging, making this data more accessible to the masses.

Happening concurrently with the rise of Trackman in the early 2000s was the tour's decision to meaningfully upgrade their shot tracking and data analytics system which eventually gave way to what is now known as ShotLink. Made possible by a large onsite team and a small army of volunteers, the tour tracks every shot made by every player each week. That feeds into a massive database that can be analyzed, spliced, and organized in a multitude of ways. Tour players were soon able to track greens in regulation, driving distance, fairways hit, average putting distance, and hundreds of other metrics. This data allowed for the discovery of new paradigms that sometimes debunked timeless adages such as, "Drive for show, putt for dough." The phrase coined by Bobby Locke, a South African golfer that won four Open Championships, became golfing wisdom passed down through the ages.[5] It was rarely questioned because, on the surface, it made a lot of sense. The putter is used far more than any other club in the bag so it would be logical to conclude it also has the greatest impact on scoring.

Through the '80s and '90s golf commentators, writers, coaches, and pros regularly extolled the supreme importance of the short game in general. Just a few examples of headline from that time period include, "The Short Answer to Lower Scores: Area pros say fastest way to cut strokes from your game is to practice, practice, practice your short game"; "Shortcut to Success: Although they tend to focus on driving, most golfers would be better served if they spent more time working on their short games"; "The short game is 65 percent of golf. If you don't have a short game, get a tennis racket."[6] The main points of argument in these articles were all too familiar including the proportion of total shots executed within 100 yards and how many greens are normally hit in regulation.

Mark Broadie, a Columbia Business School professor, realized the traditional way of benchmarking player performance was flawed. Metrics such as fairways-in-regulation, greens-in-regulation, and putts per round, upon deeper analysis, are incomparable across players and possibly even misleading. He developed the now well-known strokes-gained statistic which, in simple terms, allows every shot to be accurately compared to others in the field and expressed in stroke format. For example, everyone knows that a 300 yard drive in the fairway is better than a 280 yard drive, but how much better? Obviously, the expected score on a hole is lower the closer one is to the pin, but how much lower? Strokes gained can quantify this. Perhaps in this example, the expected score from 20 yards closer would be .15 strokes. This revolutionized the way players and coaches understood the importance of each part of the game.

A major takeaway from Broadie's research is that the long game (drives and approach shots) has a greater impact on scoring than putting and chipping when comparing oneself to the rest of the field. A key flaw in the previous thinking had been simply looking at, for example, the total number of putts taken in a round. A very large portion of those are putts within three feet, a distance with a very high make percentage. It's hard to gain a stroke on the field by improving one's proficiency in three-foot putts, there simply isn't enough dispersion in skill among players on that particular part of the game. If, however, one can improve approach shot accuracy where a meaningful dispersion in skill level is present, the opportunities to gain strokes on the field are more abundant. Amazingly, a half century old golf adage was flipped on its head when put under the microscope of advanced data. In 2011, the PGA tour officially adopted the stroke-gained metric and it immediately got used by players such as Dustin Johnson, Brandt Snedeker, Zach Johnson, and Rory McIroy.

Another golf myth that Broadie's research busted was the belief a golfer should lay up to their best approach yardage. On a par five, for example, it was previously believed a player should hit their second shot to a distance of say 90 yards from the hole, as that might set the up for a perfect, full sand wedge. The philosophy being a full swing at a comfortable yardage would result in a better score than having to hit a three-quarter or half swing shot from something closer to the hole. Like many golf myths of old, it made a lot of sense on the surface, but the data doesn't back up the strategy. Using strokes gained, a player learns they are likely to score better when hitting a 40 yard approach shot from the rough than a 90 yard full swing from the fairway.

It was this type of analysis that drove Bryson DeChambeau's strategy of ripping driver off nearly every tee during the 2020 US Open at Winged Foot. US Open fairways are notoriously narrow making even normal drives difficult to put in the short stuff. That being the case, if there's a reasonable chance a normal drive will end up in the rough, why not crush it and be in the rough 30 - 40 yards farther? It's hard to argue with the logic. Bryson was third in strokes gained off the tee all week and while that wasn't the whole story (as the rest of his game was stellar as well), it was certainly a big reason why he captured the major victory.

In today's world of smart devices, advanced statistical tracking isn't just for the pros. The average golfer can now stat their round more easily than ever before through smartwatches, clubs, and balls. Smart golf watches, for example, can sense when a player hits the ball and precisely map an entire round using GPS technology. The data is uploaded into the cloud where it can be compared to other amateur golfers of the same skill level and strokes gained metrics contrasted.

The future is exciting to contemplate. Imagine a system

in which smart golf clubs track a player's swing plane, speed, and angle of attack comparing that to the ball speed, shape, and distance logged by a smart golf ball and correlate both of those with scoring results. In a day not too distant from now, the average golfer will sit down after a round to look at their artificial intelligence golf coach app which will have crunched through their personal golf data to come up with swing change tips, course management strategy suggestions, and equipment change recommendations. The first couple generations of this technology have already hit the market in the form of virtual caddies that can make club recommendations, pinpoint the best aiming target, and calculate scoring probabilities from anywhere on a hole. While digital caddies can't be used in tournament play, the intuition gained and lessons learned from looking at the data during practice rounds effectively serve as a mental game training program far superior than simply reading a mental game book or watching a mental game video. It's hard to conceive of a system that would be more effective in training a player to make the highest probability decisions and to manage a course in a better way, than the repetition of seeing a heat map of possible outcomes backed by shot distribution data from their own swing.

Access to advanced technology and instruction will likely become imperative to maximizing a golfer's potential. South Korea, as a country, has among the best systems for connecting emerging talent with the resources necessary to succeed. The process has resulted in South Korean women dominating the LPGA Tour and many highly successful PGA Tour players. Players such as Inbee Park, Sei Young Kim, Jin Young Ko, Sung Hyun Park, and So Yeon Ryu have topped the LPGA Tour money list in recent years. When asked why South Korean women have had such success, American golfer Jessica Korda said, "Honestly, I think they have a better developmental program for juniors. The Korean girls are dominating. They have a national team. Golf is an expensive sport; they pay for that. They travel to different countries and play a bunch. I feel like one of the things that the U.S. doesn't have is a national team and somebody to help the girls and the boys kind of grow through that process."[7] In addition to a formal training structure, South Koreans have adopted technology such as launch monitors and indoor simulators much faster than other geographies. These advantages, coupled with a strong culture of hard work, persistence, and dedication, have led to dominating results and a framework for other countries to follow.

Possibly in response to situations such as these, the USGA and R&A recently announced changes to the rules for amateur status which will eliminate all sponsorship-related restrictions and allow players to benefit from their name, image, and likeness. This will create a more equal playing field for amateurs across the world in access to resources to develop, compete, and improve.

Another forum ripe for technology use is the Ryder Cup. After the stinging loss at Gleneagles, capped off by infighting and finger-pointing, the Americans and PGA realized they needed to provide better tools, data, and information to captains. The Europeans had been taking an analytical approach for years and having won eight out of the previous ten competitions, it was hard to argue with their winning formula. The Americans hosted the 2016 cup at Hazeltine and captain Davis Love teamed up with quant gurus to crunch the numbers. The first decisions Love needed to make were his captain's picks, remarking before the choice, "Our alternate shot is a big part of how we pair, how we pick. Looking at Hazeltine and how it suits certain players, I think there's going to be two obvious picks and then there's going to be two we're going to have to waffle about a little bit. The stats will help us narrow that down."[8] The home host is also responsible for setting up the course and it became clear that the Americans were not only longer off the tee, but also superior in wedge play to the Europeans which informed the course set up. Pairing players for alternate shot was ripe with opportunities to optimize and complement strengths. While Davis Love kept a lot of things close to the vest with regard to his strategy and use of data, it's obvious the efforts paid off with the Americans capturing victory for the first time since 2008.

Not to be outdone, the Europeans recaptured the Cup in 2018. Captain Thomas Bjorn (who had been helping the Europeans use statistics for years) and his consulting partner were more willing to share with fans how data drove some of their winning decisions. First, Le Golf National was chosen because it's a regular stop on the European tour, but very unfamiliar for most American players. Thick rough and an emphasis on accuracy mitigated the distance advantage of the Americans. Second, the theme on pairings was to match accurate drivers such as Henrik Stenson and Rory McIlroy with approach-shot strong Justin Rose and Ian Poulter respectively. Francesco Molinari and Tommy Fleetwood's games complemented each other so well statistically that the data suggested pairing them four times together, which in retrospect looked like a genius move as they posted a 4-0 record in those matches.[9]

The Ryder Cup could be the most fertile ground for data analytics in golf given the numerous variables over which the hosting captain has control. It appears big data is here to stay in the Ryder Cup with PGA of America CEO, Pete Bevacqua, recently saying, "Whether you're managing a Major League baseball team, you're coaching a college or NBA basketball team, NFL or college football team, the use of data, the use of analytics is so critical to have in today's sports environment."[10]

As stated at the beginning of the chapter, golf will always be a game of both art and science, but it's clear that advanced analytics is here to stay and will be an essential tool for elite and even weekend golfers going forward. When one of the most analytical minds in golf was asked whether golf was an art or science, Bryson DeChambeau summed it up best: "It is a mesh of the two, if you can beautifully mesh art and science to enhance your game, there's no downside."[11]

Out of the Box Bucket List:

- ☐ Get access to a Trackman, know your stats
- ☐ Use a launch monitor
- ☐ Use a smart golf watch
- ☐ Use smart golf clubs
- ☐ Use smart golf balls
- ☐ Track your strokes gained vs. other amateurs
- ☐ Practice your long game more than short
- ☐ Rip driver off nearly every tee
- ☐ Hit your draws with the clubface open and your fades with it closed
- ☐ Focus on clubface direction over swing path
- ☐ Never lay up to a "good yardage"
- ☐ Use a virtual caddie

CHAPTER 10
NEW FRONTIERS FOR GOLF

As mentioned earlier, one of golf's unique appeals among sports is the variability of the playing field. Not only can the same course be set up in dramatically different ways, golfers can travel to disparate parts of the world and encounter courses built on mountains, through deserts, in tropical rainforests, and on top of sand dunes, each one bringing variability and renewed interest. Even with this endless selection, that doesn't mean there aren't other, unconventional formats in which the game can be enjoyed.

The attraction of many of these alternatives is they take less time than the traditional four to five hour 18 hole golf round. Golf's governing bodies are acutely aware of the playing time problem and have focused on ways to speed up rounds. In 2015, the R&A did a global survey on playing time that included 56,000 people in 122 different countries. 60% of respondents said playing in less time would improve their enjoyment of the game, with younger age categories placing a greater emphasis on this point. Studies done by the USGA have shown as high as 75% of golfers strongly agree pace of play is critical in contributing to one's enjoyment of a round.[1]

For many years, the USGA has been championing a nationwide initiative called "Tee it Forward" which encourages golfers to play tees consistent with their skill level. In many cases it means playing forward tees, making courses shorter and easier. Jack Nicklaus has been a vocal advocate for the Tee It Forward campaign and results appear to be encouraging. Additionally, several recent rules changes are directly focused on speeding up play such as reducing the time allowed to search for a lost ball from five minutes to three; a local rule option allowing out-of-bounds shots to be dropped at the point of exit (similar to what is done with a hazard); giving players the option to putt without removing the flagstick; insisting shots be made in less than 40 seconds; and an emphasis on ready golf.

All of these efforts are well-intentioned and certainly helpful, but even in the best-case scenario they collectively might shave 15-20 minutes off the average 18 hole round. In an increasingly busy world filled with seemingly more limited attention spans, people are searching for ways to enjoy golf in a compressed time frame and in different, sometimes more captivating ways. One might suggest an obvious solution to the time dilemma is a quick nine hole jaunt, but a two hour golf round can still, in reality, be a three hour door-to-door undertaking when factoring in the need to arrive early, drive time, etc. Many of the alternative ways to enjoy golf that are gaining increasing acceptance fit within a one hour timeframe.

The second major theme in play here is the "fall of formality" over the past couple of decades, driven largely by the millennial generation, but also being adopted to varying degrees across the age spectrum.[2] In the workplace, it has taken the form of increasingly casual dress and professional interactions. Mark Zuckerberg famously wore a hoodie on Facebook's high-profile IPO roadshow, receiving backlash from executives and media alike. One market analyst commented that wearing a hoodie was "a mark of immaturity. I think that he has to realize he's bringing investors in right now, and I think he's got to show them the respect that they deserve because he's asking them for their money."[3] At the end of the day, however, the hoodie didn't stop investors then or since from pouring billions of dollars into the company.

In general, there's an aversion among millennials to playing by someone else's rules, deferring to authority, or letting a small group of people at the top dictate how everyone else must act. Golf has been experiencing its own fall of formality; country clubs have relaxed dress codes, eased protocols, and become more family/kid friendly. Once completely off limits, jeans are now permitted in 87% of private clubs to some degree. Many of the alternative ways to enjoy golf fit in the bull's eye of this "fall of formality" movement.

One of the most popular recent trends is the dramatic growth of TopGolf, an innovative concept that combines golf, socializing, and food, and can be done in as little as an hour even after the sun goes down. The massive complexes are constructed as multi-tiered driving ranges with targets and microchip-tracked golf balls that keep your score based on how accurate you hit your shots. Play occurs in somewhat of a bowling-style process, one at a time with everyone else sitting around chatting while snacking on flatbread pizza and hot wings. The company's slogan is "It's everyone's game," the not-so-subtle implication being that traditional golf is not everyone's game. Quotes from TopGolf commercials say it all – "There's no pressure to be good here," "Every shot should be celebrated," and "Whether you're a golfer or not, you will enjoy it."

The first TopGolf complex in the US was built in 2005 and the company has grown rapidly to over 60 locations worldwide. More than 14 million people will tee it up in a TopGolf facility in a year, a number that's sure to climb in the future. Roughly half of those don't play traditional golf regularly which shows the expanding reach of this innovative version of golf. An indication of its popularity is the recently televised TopGolf Championship on the Golf Channel, with regional qualifiers held worldwide and a bracket-style finale in Las Vegas.

Even professional golfers are getting in on the action with Greg Norman calling it, "a breath of fresh air for the game," and saying, "This is just what golf needs." Andrew "BEEF" Johnston said, "It's a real good family environment. I come out with my friends and family, I bring my mom out. She won't ever play golf... and she loved it... Anyone can play, it doesn't matter what level you are. I can play it, someone who's never started can play it and you can all play together." When asked about the difference between normal golf and TopGolf Hunter Mahan said, "This is fun. Golf can be brutal, it can be frustrating, it can be cruel sometimes. It's fun, you can come out here and bring your friends and family and have a good time. They make golf fun, it's a great thing."[4] Summed up, TopGolf is cheaper than a full round, takes less time to play, occurs in a more relaxed atmosphere, is enjoyed with more people, and can be played late into the night in more varied types of weather. It's not hard to understand its explosive expansion over the past 15 years. While it's easy to compare and contrast, growth in TopGolf is not mutually exclusive with that of the traditional game, the two can be symbiotic in nature if the right bridges are built.

For similar reasons as technology-enabled driving ranges, at-home simulators are becoming increasingly popular. They used to be only for the rich and famous with price tags in the tens of thousands of dollars, but technology has improved and more affordable launch monitors have made their way into the market over the past many years bringing winter and night golf into the garages and basements of the masses. For as low as a few hundred dollars, enthusiasts can shake the winter blues and have virtual access to golf courses they may never have the opportunity to play in the flesh. With a few clicks of the mouse, one can load up Augusta National, Pebble Beach, Pine Valley, or St. Andrews from the comfort of home. Every year launch monitor technology is improving to make the experience more realistic and shot predictions more accurate.

Additionally, with an internet connection, golfers across the country can play against each other and compete in virtual tournaments. A sister in Texas, a dad in Chicago, and a college roommate in Ohio can all come together to play a digital Winged Foot or Cypress Point. A golf simulator becomes a way to increase practice time and hone the swing. A young, busy professional may not have time to play nine holes or go to the range, but he or she might have 30 minutes after the kids go to bed to sneak in the basement and quench their golfing thirst.

During the 2020 COVID pandemic, BMW partnered with Trackman to put on a five-week virtual professional golf tournament for European Tour players with notable names participating such as Martin Kaymer, Lee Westwood, Sergio Garcia, and Thomas Pieters. The first virtual pro tournament in history attracted 62 tour players spread across 17 different countries and was played on the virtual courses of St. Andrews, Royal Portrush, Golfclub Muchen Eichenried, Valderrama, and Wentworth Club. Fans were able to watch streaming videos of pros playing from their golf simulator rooms, converging in the first digital competition of its kind with a first place reward of $10,000 donated to charity.

While virtual tournaments are new to professional-caliber golfers, South Korean amateurs of all skill levels have been teeing up in digital competitions for years. One of the most popular sports in South Korea is known as "screen golf" or golf played on a simulator in one of 6,000 Golfzon locations across the country. Physical golf courses are in limited supply due to land constraints which has driven demand for this virtual alternative. Amazingly, more rounds of screen golf are played each year in South Korea than real golf. 350 screen golf tournaments are held daily, obviously far surpassing the number of actual golf tournaments played in real life. It's not uncommon for a junior golfer to learn the game on screen golf for years before ever teeing it up in real life. While driven out of necessity, screen golf is cheaper and faster than traditional golf and is available 24 hours a day all year long. Perhaps South Korea will be a model for other golf markets to follow.

Another trend that naturally fits within a compressed time frame is speedgolf. A speedgolf score combines the 18 hole stroke count with the time it takes to play (or run for that matter). For most competitors, the running time accounts for roughly 40% of the total score, with the remaining 60% being the traditional 18 hole stroke count. The concept inherently solves the problem of long round times, but perhaps more importantly combines physical fitness, excitement, and new strategy. Many courses are willing to give first-of-day tee times for as little as $20 to speed golfers as a means to increase rounds without clogging up the rest of the day. Lakewood Golf Course in Los Angeles sends off a batch of six to ten speed golfers every morning which has been a win-win for everyone involved. The movement has the prospect of attracting more millennials given the greater health focus, less formal nature, and faster pace of play. Still a nascent trend, if golf's elite athletes in the professional ranks got behind the idea and helped push the cause, it could become a staple part of tee sheets across the country.

Alternatively, for those who prefer to ignore the tediousness of short game perfection, behold the World Long Drive Championship circuit, a place to bomb it out there with reckless abandon. These are extraordinarily fun events with 3.0 degree loft drivers, 4x stiff shafts, and 150 mph golf swings. Worth repeating, those possessing a kindred spirit with Arnold Palmer agree with his assessment that "There's nothing in golf more spectacular and satisfying to the soul and the senses than a perfectly long and straight drive ... a long drive is good for the ego ... I've said previously, what other people may find in poetry or in art museums I find in the flight of a good drive."

The beauty of these open-to-anyone competitions is you don't have to wear a cut-off tee shirt and be a bodybuilder to participate in the fun or to just enjoy the atmosphere and exhilaration of ripping it as hard as possible. It's easy to feel a shot of euphoria after unloading on a golf ball, connecting dead-center of the clubface, and watching it sail off into the yonder distance. The regulars at these events around the country have formed a second family that is loyally supportive of each other and always willing to let another person in the group. Aside from participating, it's also fun to watch – it's the home run derby or slam dunk competition of golf with drives that run out over 400 yards.

More than simply being fantastically fun, the techniques discovered and refined on the long drive circuit have been seeping back into PGA Tour and amateur swings. Strokes gained data has highlighted the huge advantage of hitting it a long ways off the tee which catalyzed a race for distance. The risk, however, is that very high swing speeds can also be associated with a greater propensity for injury to knees and backs. Long drive competitors have, for years, mitigated these risks by either rotating on the back of their heels or simply being completely air born at impact. Rather than fade quietly into retirement, Phil Mickelson has doubled down on new swing methods that will allow him to hit what he calls "high, nasty, straight bombs." Chief among those new methods is to rotate on his right heel through impact such that his lead foot is pointed directly at the target at the end of his swing. It's something he has discussed with long drive champion Kyle Berkshire and is a tangible example of how alternative ways to play golf can have a symbiotic relationship with the traditional game.

From alternative driving to alternative putting, another trend slowly getting some traction around the country is big hole golf, a version of traditional golf that simply uses a hole larger than the normal 4.25" cup. Generally implemented in corporate, charity, or one-day tournament settings, organizers have put cups in play ranging from 8" to as large as 15". For the average golfer, the chance of making a 20' putt is an abysmally low 6%, even for professionals it's a surprisingly low 15%. Good statistics don't exist on how these numbers change for big holes, but the anecdotal evidence suggests it's still relatively challenging, yet more enjoyable. It's easy to see how making, for example, 30% of one's 20' putts would be more fun and exciting than the current demoralizing experience of traditional golf. Larger hole sizes also increase the frequency of chip-ins around the green. In a bizarre way, a larger hole would likely re-emphasize the importance of the short game and decrease the importance of driving and approach shot accuracy, so heavily weighted in today's game per the strokes gained research of Mark Broadie referenced earlier. Beneficially, big hole golf events report a 30-45 minute reduction in playing time as the entire green routine and choreography gets shortened.

The biggest pushback comes from the traditionalist view, and even that of the golfing population more broadly, that big hole golf isn't "real golf." The governing bodies, however, could legitimize big hole golf in a heartbeat by allowing rounds played on big golf hole setups to be posted for handicap purposes. In today's analytical world, it would be easy to find algorithms that accurately convert a round played on a big hole golf course into an equivalent traditional handicap score. The current handicap system already equalizes for a variety of factors through the course and slope ratings and from each set of tees; how hard would it be to add an additional variable of cup size? In nearly every other sport, beginners are given easier setups or aids. Basketballs, footballs, and soccer balls all start out small and get bigger with increased skill concurrently with the size of the court/field, size of the hoop/end zone/goal, and number of players in the competition at a given time. Excluding the choice of tees, there is very little difference in the course set up for a beginner golfer relative to an avid one. Thinking about the concessions other sports make to their beginners, it's not such a stretch to put a larger cup in play for greater enjoyability. The long-term success of it will depend on the governing bodies making it postable for handicap purposes. Otherwise, it will likely remain relegated to the corporate and charity tournament sphere.

Lastly, for the adventurous and travel-loving, the World Ice Championships held on Greenland's small island of Uummannaq is about as unique as they come. A new course is carved every year on the fjord from the ever-changing winter landscape where hazards included spots of thin ice, icebergs, negative 50 degree wind chills, and frostbite. Red and orange balls are used in order to contrast against the bright white landscape. On a traditional golf course, players want to hit greens and fairways in regulation, but in Uummannaq you want to hit "whites" and "glareways" in regulation. The tournament has always been dependent on local ice depth conditions and has, unfortunately, been canceled more often than not for many years. Hopefully, this famous arctic tournament reclaims its yesteryear glory.

This hasn't, however, stopped ice golf tournaments from popping up in other parts of the world including in Austria, Russia, Argentina, and Vermont, Minnesota, and Michigan in the US. Likely the largest of its kind, the city of Wayzata, Minnesota holds their annual Chilly Open golf tournament every February on the frozen Wayzata Bay ice. A local tradition since 1984, nearly two thousand golfers sign up each year to take part in the friendly competition in which teams come dressed in matching outfits and costumes. Complete with corporate sponsors, a chili cook-off, and festivities from dawn to dusk, it's an unconventional way to bring the community together through golf, not entirely different in feel from a TopGolf-like experience.

The handful of common threads connecting most of these alternative ways to enjoy golf are the shorter time requirement, more relaxed feel, higher excitement level, and greater opportunity to socialize while participating. Growth in these alternatives doesn't need to be mutually exclusive with that of traditional golf, but proper bridges likely need to be built so that each version of golf can learn important lessons from the other about what attracts people to the game in today's world. In this way all forms of golf can grow successfully together.

Out of the Box Bucket List:

☐ Try TopGolf
☐ Play a round of speed golf
☐ Get a home golf simulator
☐ Participate in a virtual round of golf with friends
☐ Participate in a virtual golf tournament
☐ Play a round of big hole golf
☐ Play ice golf

CHAPTER 11
BOLD PREDICTIONS
AND CONCLUSION

Arnold Palmer famously said, "Golf is deceptively simple and endlessly complicated; it satisfies the soul and frustrates the intellect. It is at the same time rewarding and maddening – and it is without a doubt the greatest game mankind has ever invented." This book explored and analyzed some of that frustrating complexity and endless permutation, but the overarching theme was simple: the best players throughout history, and almost surely those of the future, were willing to think outside the box. They were willing to break, at least in part, the human tendency toward conformity and disregard the mockery and shame so often heaped upon those diverging from the crowd.

The changing tides of golf strategy often progress imperceptibly for spans of time measured in months and years, but the decades paint an unambiguous picture of rolling evolution. The process of adaptation to and capitalization on new opportunities and conditions commonly takes a generation's time. The death of wristy putting, emergence of flop-shot style chipping, ascent of 60+ degree wedges, and the claw grip were, for some at the time, shocking out-of-the-box responses to surging green speeds. Over the decades, however, the initial mockery gave way to interest, acceptance, and ultimately adoption.

Swing techniques historically viewed as hard-and-fast rules slowly lost their luster as individual players ascended to the top of the game using different approaches. Calvin Peete and Jordan Spieth violated the immutable left arm straight law, while Moe Norman and Bryson DeChambeau broke multiple swing plane conventions. Judy Rankins and Brooke Henderson blazed new trails for gripping the golf club, while Ray Floyd, Nancy Lopez, and Jim Furyk demonstrated the most efficient path between two points isn't always a straight line. Michelle Wie introduced the world to table-top style putting, while Lexi Thompson closed her eyes in concentration at impact, and Jordan Spieth looked at the hole during the entire stroke. Where consistency and repeatability are the objectives, it's counterintuitive that the spectrum of successful methods would be so wide, yet it has been true thus far.

At many points during the 20th century, scientists convincingly proved the benefits of health and physical fitness with regard to coordination, muscle control, and athletic performance, but it wasn't until the beginning of the 21st century that golfers were compelled to become elite athletes driven by Tiger Woods and Annika Sorenstam. A handful had capitalized earlier including Bernhard Langer and Greg Norman, but it still took ~25 years from the date of Gary Player's first published book on golf fitness for it to become the norm on tour.

A golfing sage in more ways than one, Gary Player said of the mental game in 1971, "Mind is what matters and Arnold Palmer and Jack Nicklaus have great minds... In 30 years there will be 50 books on the mind to every 5 on golf theory. We are only just scratching the surface now."[1] While the prognosticated proportion of book sales might not have been exactly correct, the predicted importance of the mental game was spot on including the timeframe for acceptance. Roughly 30 years after that comment, the late '90s and early 2000s were characterized by a boom in golf psychology books led most prominently by Bob Rotella's research and writings. There were resources for mental game improvement before that time for forward thinkers, but they required intentional effort to find.

It could be argued that recent adoption cycles have shortened, yet they still are measured in double-digit years. Players like Michelle Wie, Anna Nordqvist, Tiger Woods, Justin Rose, and Hunter Mahan were all quick adopters of Trackman, but even six years after the launch of this revolutionary technology, only 30% of tour players owned one. The full adoption cycle, even in today's world, was a remarkable 10-15 years. The concurrent data revolution, backed by the tour's ShotLink system, debunked old myths and coaches uncovered new insights about the golf swing. Decades-old truisms, such as "Drive for show, putt for dough," were flipped completely upside down. Golfers such as Bryson DeChambeau are taking advantage of these new insights while others sit complacently or stubbornly in their old ways.

The obvious question now is where does the golfing world go from here? Below are six bold predictions about the future of golf. Most are forecast to occur in 15-25 years because history shows that it usually takes the rising generation to supplant old methods.

Bold Predictions about the Future

1) A switch-hitting golfer will win a professional tournament within 25 years.

2) Golfers will increasingly play opposite conventional handedness. This will manifest itself within 20 years by 25% of tour players playing left-handed, up from the current low single digits.

3) Single-length iron penetration will exceed 50% adoption among professionals within 15 years, up from the current sub 1% level.

4) Just as the wristy putting style of old perished, a similar trend will occur in the full swing. Players will use dramatically less wrist movement in 15 years. In conjunction, grips will double or triple in size from the current state for irons and woods.

5) Three and four irons will all but vanish from tour players' bags enabled by strength training and 30% of pros will carry a 64-degree wedge in 15 years, up from the current sub 5% level.

6) While less quantifiable, big data and technology will become more important than even our current expectations for swing analysis and tournament preparation. Even the most forward thinkers in this respect will likely be taken by surprise at data and technology's crucial role in a golfer's success 10 years from now.

The conceivable paths and evolution of golf from here are exciting to contemplate and will be fascinating to witness. While it's never been just about physical talent, strength, or coordination, golf has increasingly become a game of wits, the ability to out-think, out-prepare, and out-maneuver opponents before ever setting foot on the first tee. Hopefully, the lessons from these pages opened our minds to novel ways and methods of playing golf and generated ideas for bringing renewed interest, challenge, and variety to the game. Perhaps there were even a few epiphanies and paradigm shifts along the way.

The exciting part begins now – the personal experimentation, trial and error, and testing of these and your own ideas. The figurative new mountain to climb has been placed before you. For the average golfer who has been trying to get better for years without success, perhaps it is time to climb that mountain, think outside the box, experiment with unconventional ways to improve as well as new ways to enjoy the game. For aspiring collegiate and professional golfers, it will be difficult to outpace the herd by following in the tired and well-trodden paths of others. From high handicap to low, every golfer can benefit from spending time out of the box.

Out of the Box Bucket List

Putting:
- ☐ Use a cross-handed grip
- ☐ Use a palm to palm or prayer grip
- ☐ Use a claw grip
- ☐ Use a long putter
- ☐ Try side-saddle putting
- ☐ Try one-handed putting
- ☐ Try arm-lock putting
- ☐ Putt while looking at the hole
- ☐ Putt with your eyes closed
- ☐ Putt with quiet eye technique
- ☐ Try table-top putting
- ☐ Carry a stimpmeter, know the green speeds

Chipping:
- ☐ Put a 60 degree wedge in the bag
- ☐ Put a 64+ degree wedge in the bag
- ☐ Try cross-handed chipping
- ☐ Try one-handed chipping

Full Swing Grip:
- ☐ Use a baseball grip
- ☐ Use very firm grip pressure
- ☐ Use an extremely strong grip
- ☐ Use a double-overlap grip
- ☐ Grip the club 2-3 inches down from the top

Full Swing Grip:
- ☐ Start with the clubhead a foot behind the ball
- ☐ Address the ball with a very wide stance
- ☐ Set up with an extremely open stance

- ☐ Raise your hands just before takeaway
- ☐ Use very little wrist cock
- ☐ Try a one-plane swing
- ☐ Use a ¾ swing
- ☐ Swing past parallel
- ☐ Swing with the left arm bent
- ☐ Swing as hard as possible on every shot
- ☐ Use a chicken wing at impact
- ☐ Jump off the ground at impact
- ☐ Sway your hips through impact
- ☐ Swing such that you barely take a divot
- ☐ Find a way to hold off the club through impact
- ☐ Finish with the hands pointed toward the target
- ☐ Purposely hit a 30 yard fade or draw off the tee
- ☐ Use a 48" driver

Game Changers:
- ☐ Experiment golfing opposite conventional handedness
- ☐ Try switching hitting through the full bag
- ☐ Carry one opposite handed wedge
- ☐ Try switch putting with a double faced putter
- ☐ Putt opposite the rest of your bag

Equipment:
- ☐ Play a round with single-length irons
- ☐ Use cavity-back clubs for 3-6 iron and blades for the 5-9 iron.
- ☐ Put two drivers in play
- ☐ Put four wedges in play
- ☐ Pull two long irons out of the bag
- ☐ Use a fat grip putter
- ☐ Use fat grips on irons and woods
- ☐ Try counterweight grips
- ☐ Try counterweight shafts

☐ Leave the flagstick in all round

Health:
☐ Believe health impacts your golf score
☐ Make weight lifting and cardio an important golf preparation routine
☐ Combine core stability with other exercises in your workout
☐ Cross train with other sports to improve golf
☐ Eat healthy foods
☐ Avoid alcohol
☐ Try Tom Brady style workouts: pliability & resistance band emphasis
☐ Employ low weight, high rep workout regimes

Mental Game:
☐ Spend 30 minutes visualizing a round before playing
☐ Visualize each shot before hitting it
☐ Use personal triggers for increased concentration
☐ Talk to yourself during the round in a positive way
☐ Stretch like Miguel or Sedena
☐ Read putts like Camilo
☐ Take a deep breath before every shot
☐ Wear a red shirt, shorts, and hat to your next tournament
☐ Practice controlling the transition between parasympathetic and sympathetic states using brain training software
☐ Practice *pranayama* or breathing techniques as a normal pattern of life

Data, Analytics, and Strategy:
☐ Get access to a Trackman, know your stats
☐ Use a launch monitor
☐ Use a smart golf watch
☐ Use smart golf clubs
☐ Use smart golf balls

- ☐ Track your strokes gained vs. other amateurs
- ☐ Practice your long game more than short
- ☐ Rip driver off nearly every tee
- ☐ Hit your draws with the clubface open and your fades with it closed
- ☐ Focus on clubface direction over swing path
- ☐ Never lay up to a "good yardage"
- ☐ Use a virtual caddie

Alternative Ways to Enjoy Golf:
- ☐ Try TopGolf
- ☐ Play a round of speed golf
- ☐ Get a home golf simulator
- ☐ Participate in a virtual round of golf with friends
- ☐ Participate in a virtual golf tournament
- ☐ Play a round of big hole golf
- ☐ Play ice golf

Key Takeaway: Experiment with new, unconventional, and innovative methods!

REFERENCES

Introduction:
1) Woods, Tiger, The Tour Championship Press Conference 2018
2) Schupak, Adam. "Hall of Fame: Bob Charles" USA Today, 26 Feb 2002, golfweek.usatoday.com

Chapter 1:
1) Fields, Bill, "Masters Report: Thoughts from Augusta" Golf Digest, 14 April 2008
2) Low, George. The Master of Putting. Collier Macmillan, 1983
3) McDermott, Barry. "The Putter God Forgot" Sports Illustrated, 18 June 1979, vault.si.com.
4) "Orville Moody known for effortless, consistent swing" The Joplin Globe, 14 Oct 2017. Joplinglobe.com
5) "1969 US Open Champion Orville Moody Dies" golf.com
6) Hox, Doc. "Necessity is the Mother of Invention" Arizona Golfer, July 2013, azgolfernew.com
7) Hafner, Dan. "US Senior Open: Daughter's Reading Lesson Fuels Moody" LA Times. 3 July 1989. Latimes.com
8) USGA & R&A. "Anchoring the club – Understanding Proposed Rule" 27 Nov 2012. Usga.org
9) USGA & R&A. "Explanation of Decision to Adopt Rule 14-1b of the Rules of Golf" 21 May 2013
10) Mayo, Michael. "Putting Problem Has Long Answer, But Not All Agree." SunSentinel. 6 Mar 1991
11) Verdi, Bob. "Lietzke has no Interest in being Golf's Top Banana" Chicago Tribune. 27 Oct 1994
12) Diaz, Jaime. "Gone Fishin' for Bruce Lietzke, Time off is the Secret to the Wonderful Life he has at Home and on the PGA Tour" Sports Illustrated 22 May 1995. Vault.si.com
13) McGarr, Rob. "What do tour pros look at when putting." Today's Golfer. 23 Feb 2016. Todaysgolfer.co.uk.com
14) Vickers, Joan N. "Neuroscience of the Quiet Eye in Golf Putting." University of Calgary. 2012

Chapter 2:
1) "How fast is the green? Thanks to Ed Stimpson, we now Know" Cape Cod Times, 6 June 1998.
2) McCabe, Jim. "The Real History of Edward Stimpson's Special Gift: The Stimpmeter" Golfweek.com
3) "Why you should try a 64-degree Wedge" Golf.com
4) Owen, David. "The Yips, What's behind the condition that every golfer dreads." The New Yorker. 26 May 2014. Newyorker.com
5) Carter, Lain. "Jason Palmer: European Tour card secured with one-handed chipping." BBC Sports. 4 Nov 2014. Bbc.com 12 June 1985

Chapter 3:
1) O'Brien, Jim. USGA Films – 1962 US Open
2) Parascenzo, Marino. USGA Films – 1962 US Open
3) Golf Channel Academy short video
4) Shirley, Billy. "Whom can the golf pro turn to?: Most of the top players have own teachers. Even the heavyweights need help when the fall out of the Groove." LA Times.
5) Floyd, Raymond. "My Shot: Raymond Floyd" Golf Digest. 4 June 2018
6) Yocom, Guy. "My Shot: Moe Norman" Golf Digest. 7 July 2007
7) 1994 Moe Norman golf swing demo, youtube.com
8) Penick, Harvey. "For All Who Love the Game: Lessons and Teachings for Women" 1999
9) Pileggi, Sarah. "With a Grip on Glory and her Game" Sports Illustrated. 6 Jun 1997. Vault.si.com
10) Eubanks, Steve. "The Memorial Celebrates Golf's True Friend in Judy Rankins" 28 May 2019

11) Seitz, Nick. "How to Improve Your Golf Swing: Watch Snead" The New York Times. 5 May 1974
12) McDermott, Barry. "A Long Shot out of a trap." Sports Illustrated. 24 Mar 1980
13) "The Long Journey of Calvin Peete" The New York Times 3 Jan 1983
14) Weber, Bruce. "Calvin Peete, 71, a Racial Pioneer on the PGA Tour, Is Dead"
15) Nichols, Beth Ann. "Nancy Lopez took LPGA by storm, but will we see another like her" 31 Mar 2019
16) Nancy Lopez Golf, youtube.com
17) Talk the Talk: Jim Furyk's Essential Golf Lessons, The Dan Patrick Show. Youtube.com
18) Tadman, Joel. "Bubba Watson Q&A: I've Never had a Lesson" Golf Monthly. 3 July 2019
19) "Why Jordan Spieth's Weird Swing Works So Well" 10 July 2017 youtube.com
20) Stanley, Adam. "Brooke Henderson shares secret to her booming tee shots" thescore.com
21) Stevenson, Chris. "Golf Her Way: On Brooke Henderson's Formula for Success" 27 Aug 2018. Flagstick.com
22) Lavner, Ryan. "Validation for DeChambeau: Did it my way" 17 July 2017 Golfchannel.com

Chapter 4:
1) "Epigenetic regulation of lateralized fetal spinal gene expression underlies hemispheric asymmetries" Ruhr University Bochum, Germany. 1 Feb 2017
2) Ooki, Syuichi. "An overview of human handedness in twins" US National Library of Medicine, National Institute of Health 2014
3) Vallortigara, Giorgio. "Handedness: What Kangaroos Tell Us about our Lopsided Brains" University of Trento, Piazza della Manifattura, Italy. 3 Aug 2015
4) Giljov, Andrey. "Parallel Emergence of True Handedness in the Evolution of Marsupials and Placentals" Saint Petersburg State University, Russia. 11 March 2015
5) Bryden, P.J. "A new method of administering the Grooved Pegboard Test: performance as a function of handedness and sex" Dec 2004
6) "Handedness and Asymmetry of Motor Skills Learning in Right-handers" Seoul University College of Medicine, Seoul, Korea. 20 June 2006.
7) Scharoun, Sara. "Hand preference, performance abilities, and hand selection in children" University of Waterloo, Canada. 18 Feb 2014
8) "The Success of Sinister Right-Handers in Baseball" New England Journal of Medicine
9) Lau Jr., Charley. "Lau's Laws on Hitting: The Art of Hitting .400 for the Next Generation" 2000
10) Knapik GG, Marras WS. Spine loading at different lumbar levels during pushing and pulling. Ergonomics. 2009 Jan; 52(1): 60-70
11) Brooks, Bussiere, Jennions. "Sinister strategies succeed at the Cricket World Cup" March 2004
12) onearmgolf.org
13) Local CBS News Spotlight on Fightmaster Cup
14) O'Connor, Ian. "Keeping Score" USA Today 15 Aug 2005
15) Hazeltine, Rick. "In His Father's Image: Mickelson Learned Golf Backwards, but Career is on Fast Forward." 8 July 1989
16) Eden, Scott. "Stroke of Madness" ESPN.com. 22 Jan 2013
17) Sherman, Ed. "How it all began." Chicago Tribune 4 July 2001
18) Kingdom Magazine, Issue 16, March 22, 2010
19) Schupak, Adam. "Hall of Fame: Bob Charles" USA Today. 26 Feb 2002
20) V, Rick. "A Conversation with Titleist Brand Ambassador Brian Harman." 4 Jan 2019. Titleist.com
21) "Erica Shepherd Aims Repeat Title" Indystar.com 14 July 2018
22) Sickle, Gary Van. "Hefty Lefties not long ago left-handed golfers were taken lightly. Today a half dozen of them are throwing their weight around on tour." 12 March 2001 vault.si.com
23) "Big swing to the left" The Irish Times 4 July 2000
24) "First Lady" Chron 21 Jan 2002
25) World Golf Hall of Fame Induction speech
26) Greg Norman interview with Butch Harmon

27) "Great Golf Swings: Johnny Miller", 21 Jan 2010. learningagoodgolfswing.blogspot.com
28) Henrikstenson.com
29) Nelson, Byron. "From the Inside Out" 2018 Fulton Books, Inc.

Chapter 5:
1) Boyette, John. "Why do lefties do so well at August?" 8 April 2015 augusta.com
2) Feherity interview with Phil Mickelson
3) "Augusta Champions on why Golden Bell is carnage" nationalclubgolfer.com
4) Masters press interview
5) Personal interview with Ed Mate
6) Dorman, Larry. "From left to right, the putt most feared" The New York Times. 1 May 2011
7) Fairbank, Dave, "Switch-hitting Golfer is feeling baseball fever" 9 July 1992. Daily Press

Chapter 6:
1) Bryson DeChambeau Talks F7 One Length Irons, Cobra Puma Golf, youtube.com
2) 2016 Masters Press Conference – Bryson DeChambeau
3) Schupak, Adam. "Golf Pro Aims to Revolutionize an Industry with One-Size-Fits-All Irons" 28 Jan 2017.
4) "Why 14 Clubs" linksmagazine.com
5) Johnson, Mike. "Did you know: The origins of the 14-club limit" 7 April 2020
6) Tursky, Andrew. "Gear Talk with Tom Kite: The first 60-degree wedge ever." 10 Mar 2020 golf.com
7) Wall, Jonathan. "Choi's fat putter grip started major trend." 4 Aug 2014 pgatour.com
8) Cobra demo day clinic, youtube.com
9) Silverberg, Tran, Adams. "Optimal Targets for the Bank Shot in Men's Basketball" 2011 North Carolina State University.

Chapter 7:
1) Harig, Bob. "At 80, Gary Player still fit as ever" 31 Oct 2015 ESPN.com
2) Murray, Jim, "Whatever happened to the fat kid who used to beat Arnie?" LA Times 3 Nov 1985
3) Mell, Randall, "19th hole cause for many three putts" 4 March 2012 golfchannel.com
4) Hansen, Ernst. "Improved marathon performance by in-race nutritional strategy intervention." 5 June 2014
5) Hottenrott, Kuno. "A scientific nutrition strategy improves time trial performance by ≈6% when compared with a self-chosen nutrition strategy in trained cyclists: a randomized cross-over study." 16 May 2012
6) "Obesity: Facts, Figures, Guidelines" West Virginia wvdhhr.org.
7) "How diabetes causes muscle loss" Kobe University 22 Feb 2019
8) "More Muscle Means Better Regulation Of Blood Pressure" Medical College of Georgia 26 Nov 2004
9) Jong-Hyuck Kim, Wi-Young So "Association between overweight/ obesity and academic performance in South Korean Adolescents" 2013
10) "Hypertension, Obesity escalate memory loss in people at risk for alzheimer's disease" 14 Nov 2018 Alzheimer's Disease Research Center.
11) Augusta Chronicles 7 Jan 2000
12) Johnson, Roy "From Cub to Man: Tiger Reveals His Workout Routine" 29 June 2007 ESPN.com
13) The Big Miss, Hank Haney
14) Cromley, Janet. "To build power – and prevent injury – golfers work the core." LA Times 2 April 2007
15) LaRosa, Frank. "Meet Anika Sorenstam" Sacramento Magazine 26 April 2007
16) Michelle G. Swainson, Alan M. Batterham, Costas Tsakirides, Zoe H. Rutherford, Karen Hind. Prediction of whole-body fat percentage and visceral adipose tissue mass from five anthropometric variables.
17) Cason, Christopher. "The Real-life diet of Dustin Johnson, The World's Most Jacked Golfer" 15 Feb 2008. GQ
18) Wildenradt, Reegan. "Brooks Koepka is One of the Fittest Guys in Golf – Here's How He Does It." 2 Feb 2018. Mens Health

19) Palmer, Arnold. A Life Well Played

20) Brady, Tom. TB12 Method: How to Achieve a Lifetime of Sustained Peak Performance

Chapter 8:

1) Hutchinson, Alex. "Angry coaches beware: Athletes respond poorly to negative feedback, studies find" The Globe and Mail 19 May 2012

2) TED Talk, Alex Honnald

3) Smith, Dave. "Beating the Bunker: The Effect of PETTLEP imagery on golf bunker shot performance." Oct 2008

4) Whitworth, Kathy. "Kathy Whitworth's Little Book of Golf Wisdom" 2007

5) Nicklaus, Jack. Golf My Way. 2007

6) Game Like Training "Golf Psychology - Jason Day explains his pre-shot routine - Golf's Mental Game" youtube.com

7) Haynes, John. "Sam Snead on Golf's Most Underrated Move". 31 Oct 2015 johnhaynesgolf.blogspot.com

8) Mack, Mickey Gay. "Effects of preshot rountine time and movements on free throw shooting performance" 1991

9) Glick, Shav. "Bradley has ring of success" LA Times 7 April 1986

10) Magone, David. "What is Pranayama" Gaia 13 Sept 2016

11) Perciavalle, Corrado "The Role of Deep Breathing on Stress."

12) Ma, Yue, Gong, Zhang, Duan, Shi, Wei, Li "The Effect of Diaphragmatic Breathing on Attention, Negative Affect and Stress in Healthy Adults" Beijing University & Massachusetts General Hospital 6 June 2017

13) Hartsell, Jeff. "How U.S. star Lexi Thompson gains perspective from Wounded Warriors" The Post and Courier 27 May 2019

14) Hill, Russell Dr. "Red Advantage in Sports" Durham University https://community.dur.ac.uk/r.a.hill/red_advantage.htm

15) Connolly, Rendlemen "Dominance, Intimidation, and Choking on the PGA Tour" Journal of Quantitative Analysis January 2009

16) Peary, Danny. "Great Golf: Essential Tips from History's Top Golfers" 2012

17) 1994 Moe Norman golf swing demo - Interview - (Part 2 of 2), youtube.com

Chapter 9:

1) Young, Adam. "Golf Geeks: The Ball Flight Laws of Golf" 2 June 2016

2) TrackMan session with Justin Rose and Sean Foley, youtube.com

3) Bobbit, Brian. Product Reviews: Trackman 29 March 2013

4) Grissett, Bob. "On the PGA Tour with Trackman, Why the world's best players rely on the device." 23 Jan 2020. GolfTips Magazine

5) PGA tour tournament interview, 1 Dec 2011

6) Aug 21, 1997; Tampa Bay Times July 30, 1998; Forth Worth Start Telegram, April 14, 1998, The Daily Oklahoman, Apri 10, 1994

7) Cunningham, Kevin. "Why do Koreans dominate Americans on the LPGA? Jessica Korda has an idea" 1 Aug 2018

8) Harig, Bob. "Assessing chances for potential Ryder Cup captains picks" 10 Sept 2016 EPSN.com

9) Wooster, Blaine. "How Analytics Helped Reclaim the Ryder Cup for Europe" 12 Nov 2018 leadersinsports.com

10) Smits, Garry. "PGA Tour makes more modifications to Stadium Course's 12th hole" 21 Feb 2018

11) 2016 Masters Press Conference – Bryson DeChambeau

Chapter 10:

1) Last, Jon "Tracking Research" Sports and Leisure Research Group

2) Belmonte, Clair. "The Fall of Formality: Why Millenials Audiences Love Casual CTAs" 13 July 2017 LinkedIn

3) "Facebook Hoodie Angers Bankers" 10 May 2012 lingq.com

4) PGA Pro Hunter Mahan in Allen Topgolf | Grand Opening Party | Topgolf youtube.com

Conclusion:

1) Star Phoenix Newspaper, June 12, 1971, Player a man of firm belief

Made in the USA
Middletown, DE
20 April 2021